Does My Bass L

The Antipoet: tl
by Paul I

Edited by Donna Daniels-Moss
(With bass lines and added anecdotes by The Bass Whore)

This book is dedicated to
Ian Newman
for a decade of abuse.

"Great bass player; he's genius."
—Ed Tudor Pole, July 2010

Black Pear Press

Does My Bass Look Big In This?
The Antipoet: the first ten years

First published 2018
by Black Pear Press Limited
www.blackpear.net

Edited by: Black Pear Press & Donna Daniels-Moss
(With bass lines and added anecdotes by The Bass Whore)

The moral right of the author has been asserted.

ISBN 978-1-910322-71-0

Cover photos by Ian Newman
Cover design by Elliott O'Brart—obrart.co.uk
The Antipoet logo created by Paul Solomons—paulsolomons.co.uk

Foreword—Does My Bass Look Big In This?

By Carole Matthews

I first came across The Antipoet at the Waterside Festival in Costa del Keynes. We were, somewhat unfortunately, booked in the same slot. The Organiser and I both looked over at the two burly and slightly terrifying guys in punk gear and it was suggested that I should be the one to sort out the mess while The Organiser beat a hasty retreat.

I could see why. He obviously had as little experience as I did of remonstrating with gentlemen in bondage trousers. If possible, their manager looked even more fierce. I wasn't even sure why a lady romance novelist of sensitive disposition and punk poets were even on the same stage. The Organiser had a lot to answer for. Filled with trepidation, I girded my loins and explained that there had been a mistake. Would it be possible for me to go first as I had a later engagement? Would they mind awfully? With the kind hearts and generosity of spirit that is (very occasionally) seen in their poetry, they agreed.

I did my reading and, instead of going off to my prior commitment, I was intrigued enough to stay and listen to The Antipoet set. I was blown away. Great poetry, a unique style, subversive material. I'd never seen anything like it and I loved it. So did everyone else. They had the crowd in their hands. You should have been there! If I'd had to follow that, I'd have run away to hide.

That was it. I became a firm fan, going along to many gigs in the years since. I've learned that as well as being an excellent bard, scary Paul likes fine wine and goats, but doesn't eat them. I know that Ian is as comfortable being Diane. And their manager isn't fierce at all. Actually, she is.

So, congratulations on a wonderful decade of wittily incisive poetry, muddy fields, chemical toilets and playing for food. I'm sure that all your fans past, present and future, will hope as much as I do that there's a lot more to come.

Contents

1. The Stabbing Pub

**"An act at the forefront of the new movement, with material
dripping in parody. They take poetry to a new level, with
performances as memorable as they are hilarious"**
—The Stage, July 2010

'For every action there is an equal and opposite reaction...'

Someone clever once said that, back in the days when there were
still clever things left to say.

To my mind, The Antipoet is one such reaction. We didn't sit down
and plan this whole thing out, you know; neither of us had done
anything like this before: we were serious musicians! It just happened;
we slipped'n fell.

The Antipoet was intended as a spontaneous act of lyrical terrorism:
a reaction; a rebellion in poetic terms; hence the overtly provocative
moniker.

'Poetry?' I hear you cry, 'hang about: we thought you were
comedians!'

No. We do poetry and no, we're not ashamed of that. Poetry is what
we do whether you like that sort of thing or not. We make words rhyme.
Ish. Alright, in an apparently comedic way and with the benefit of a
rockin' double bass accompaniment, but there's no hiding from our
apparently unfashionable remit: WE DO POETRY AT PEOPLE...

...just not necessarily the type of poetry that you may have been fearing,
when suddenly, in between bands in the middle of a pumping punk
festival, the MC nervously mounts the stage to declare: 'And now,
boys'n girls, we've got a rare treat f'you all; please put yer 'ands together
an' welcome—a poet!'

There have been those who have suggested that we ought to 'play down' the poetry angle:

'Y'shouldn't sell y'selves short,' a comedian once told us; convinced that he was bestowing upon us the greatest of compliments, whilst also doing us a huge marketing favour in the process, 'don't tell 'em it's poetry,' he went on, 'you'll frighten people away. You wanna' brand y'selves as "musical comedy".'

We have actually found ourselves billed as "a band" on more than one occasion by promoters who, whilst happy to put us on, have been reputationally wary of telling their regular punters the whole horrible truth of what they've actually booked for them.

So let's get it out in the open now, before you get too far in and find yourself enjoying rhyming couplets and ranty, syncopated verse for its own sake; before you get corrupted by this pair of middle-aged; middle classed, Camden Leisure Pirates and find yourself admitting that you like… poetry! Let us unmask the masquerading pachyderm in the room before an American dentist has the chance to stalk'n shoot it—

You have just bought/ borrowed/ stolen (delete as applicable)… A POETRY BOOK!

Singer, author, compere and shouty loudmouth poet, Paul Eccentric, (that's me, by the way: the one with the pen) and omnipresent bass player for hire, Ian Newman (the one with the penchant for lace), met at an open mic night in what was colloquially known as 'The Stabbing Pub' in High Wycombe in February 2007. Ian had already assumed the mantle of Bass Whore by this point; shamelessly offering himself out for any and every wandering wannabe turn that showed up to strut their frustrated stuff and who might not have previously realised they required bass backing. 'Y'gunna need bass on that,' being one of the first things one heard on entering said establishment, armed with one's battered old guitar, low self-esteem and suitcase containing every effects peddle known to man and a few they'd made up.

I, on the other hand—a singer whose back catalogue sales had been suffering a temporary dip, shall we say—had found myself reduced to

2

prostituting my own art by murdering covers of songs that I barely knew (just, I might add, in order 'to keep a hand in'), when it was brought to my attention that the lady who ran the night—hated poetry. Sadly, I can't remember now how I discovered this stray fact; sadly, because it turned out to be one of those pivotal moments in both Ian's and my lives and it would have added a bit of colour to this worn old anecdote.

Thinking about it now, though, 'hated' is probably a little harsh. She didn't really hate 'poetry', she just hated the idea of poets turning up at her gig and ruining her 'eclectic mix' of hasbeen musicians and neverwere singer-cum-shouters. It lowered the tone, apparently; it wasted time; bored the punters and it was also something of a public health risk: this place having a well-earned, violent reputation to uphold.

I had, in a previous life, dabbled with the art of performance poetry and had been looking for an excuse to give it another shot and so, armed with this tempting titbit, along with a desperate need to get back to original material as quickly as possible, was thus inspired to get back on the horse and give it another kick!

The more she disliked giving stage space to my ranty poetry, the more I enjoyed encouraging others to join me in my endeavour to piss her off. It wasn't that I didn't like her—we were mates, we'd sung in a band together and she'd been hassling me to come down and join in for months—it's just that the anarchist in my soul has always hated people laying down rules that make no rational sense. WHY did it all have to be music and why did it all have to be covers? Who says that nobody likes poetry? It'd said 'OPEN MIC' in the window; surely, then, an 'anything goes' policy is implied, no?

'Poetry's alright now and again,' she told me and my new mate Terry one night, whilst attempting to persuade me to sing and him to take his carrier bag full of future classics of the genre and go away, 'but nobody wants to hear it every week.' Well, I knows a challenge when I hears one.

The muse thus installed, I was suddenly on a roll; cynical ravings

3

pouring forth from my subconscious mind as if a metaphorical dam had been ruptured within me, but in my haste to get it all down, I found myself reusing the same easy rhythms and tired old time signatures over and again.

Enter Ian: the man who just couldn't help himself, who offered to write me a clutch of bass riffs to hold in my head whilst I was composing.

There was only one flaw in this diabolical plan and that was that I have a dyslexic's memory for sequences and so with the words duly written around his meandering hooks, I found myself unable to remember which riff I'd written which piece to!

Thus, The Antipoet was born; Ian offering to play along behind me whilst I tripped over his bass lines.

(For the record and, seeing as how this book is supposed to be explaining the evolution of this unplanned and uninvited act, this first line up also featured our friend and occasional Antipoet depper Steve Joy on guitar and poet and author of really complicated textbooks Ilia Avroutine on drums, along with Ian and me, making it up as we went along.)

Following this, our impromptu debut and having realised that we had inadvertently created a new 'Blockheadsesque' band rather than the 'beat poetry combo' that we'd intended, we pruned ourselves back to a duo and The Antipoet that you now know and begrudge was born.

I did have to persuade him to buy, learn to play and carry around a double bass, though… just because it looked better in silhouette than his Fender and for no better reason!

Soon after that, The Stabbing Pub closed. (Nothing to do with us or the poetry, I'm told.) Unperturbed, our merry band of open mic misfits, namely: ourselves, Poeterry, parodist Philfy Phil, The Artwist and Steve'n Jen, set off on a mission to mix up other open mics in the area; though it was to be a short-lived tour, as it soon became clear to us just how generous our previous host had actually been!

Nobody wanted us. We were too old and too 'weird' for the home counties open mic circuit, apparently. So, off we went to find a proper poetry gig…

Poetry Promoter: 'The Antipoet? What are y'then, anti-poetry?'
—No. Antipoetry is a poetic movement that merely eschews the formal rules and conventions of mainstream poetry.
'Well, If y'don' like it, why d'y'wanna gig at a poetry night?'
—We're poets.
'We? What, so there's more'n one a ya'?'
—We're a duo.
'Why d'y'need two a ya's t'do poetry?'
—It's a choice thing. We're beat poets. He slaps the bass and I do the talking.
'So it's not poetry then; it's music. Tha's why y'the antipoets?'
—The Antipoet.
'But there's two've ya'! Nah, y'not f'r us, son; we only book proper poets, 'ere; poets we've 'EARD of; poets wiv' a university educassion. You wanna try a music pub.'

Music Promoter: 'I'm sorry; you're the who?'
—No, We're The Antipoet.
'Poets? No, sorry; we don't book poets in here; this is a music venue.'
—We were told we couldn't be poets because we use a double bass.
'A double bass, you say? Oh, right. Well, we'll give y'a listen then…
'Mmmm…
'Nah, that's not music, mate; that's y'comedy y'doing there. Nah, nah, nah! The punters in here'll skin y'alive if they think yer taking the piss. Nah, boys. You need to try a comedy club.'

Comedy Promoter: 'The Antipoet, you say?'
—That's us.
'Bit of a funny name for a stand-up, isn't it?'

—Thought that was the idea?

'Well, tell us a joke, then.'

—A joke?

'Yeah; y'know: baddaboom baddaboom, boom tish.'

—We're more… 'lyrical' funny.

'You're poets, aren't ya'! I knows a bleedin' poet when I 'ears one! They come round 'ere tryin' a'be all 'clever-funny'; thinkin' they can rhyme a laugh outa' people; well it won't work, son! Not in 'ere, it won't. Our punters're discernin'. They c'n tell a punch line from a poet's whine.'

—But the Poetry Society won't have anything t'do with us!

'Tell ya' what, boys; come back on Tuesday. It's our slow night. We let all sorts'a weirdos in on a Tuesday. As long as you don't make a noise and disturb the Dungeons and Dragons boys or the ladies from the local coven or the canasta squad. You can use the space behind the barrels down in the cellar. It's the best offer you're goin' t'get f'that shite!'

We could have stopped there; many have said that we really should have done…

'You're shit!' said Attila The Stockbroker: famous poet of three decades standing; long admired, at the time by both of us, as it happened; midway through a gig at The Camden Eye, Camden, on the 17th of November 2010. (I understand that he's since grown to like us, though; well, he booked us for his own Glastonwick gig in 2016, anyway.)

"I might not agree with the sentiment, but you said it well"
—The Mayor of Milton Keynes, January 2015

10th anniversary drawing 2018 (Samantha Sweetland)

Backed by The Southampton Ukulele Jam 2016 (Donna Ray)

Camp Bestival Kids Stage 2016 (Thomas H Green)

8

2. Gi's Us A Gig

**"Enigmatic beat poetry. A dazzling display of poetry, comedy
and music. sometimes all in the same moment!"**
—Edinburgh Fringe Review, August 2010

As should be obvious to you by now, though, we've never taken our
critics' put downs in the way that they were intended. It's a lesson that
we learnt a long time ago. Heckles'n jibes are fuel to a poet: it's where
we get our inspiration. So come on: twatter away; hit us with your one
hundred and forty foaming-spittle characters. I'm an anarchist with a
pen; I'm not constrained by your corporate rules; I can write as many
pages as I want in lyrical response!

By December 2008 it had become apparent that no one was ever going
to offer us any work this side of The Rapture. I'd had a similar problem
with promoters and venues back in the mid nineteen eighties whilst
playing in genre-non-specific bands at a time when style affiliation and
brand identification were the be-all and end-all, so I knew how this sort
of thing worked. People are frightened of the unalike: things, people
and ways of being that they don't understand. It's a basic human
survival instinct. If it doesn't conform to type, then hit it with a big stick
'til it does, then dig yourself a hole and hide your head, just in case you
didn't hit it hard enough and it comes back to bite you.

We'd reached an impasse, Ian and I, with our not-quite-poetry, not-
really-music and occasionally funny entertainment type 'thing'. Nobody
wanted to know us; let alone book us.

Enter Donna, our handler, wrangler and oftentimes carer: the brains
of the outfit; 'The Ginger Superior' as she has since become known.

Very few of the poets that we know have 'management'. Some will
SAY that they have and will then pass you Donna's number in the vain

9

hope that she won't mind them 'assuming', but most will just tell you that it seems a bit 'excessive' for a poet and 'we can manage ourselves, thank you very much'.

Well we can't. We're Artistes, not real boys; never confuse the two! I couldn't even find my eyeliner if it wasn't in Donna's handbag, let alone work out how to apply for a festival stage using one of they computery things with all the buttons! If Donna hadn't volunteered to take on the business side of things, then he and I would still be sitting in 2008, bemoaning the fact that nobody loves us.

With the addition of her input, however—she being the sensible, logical tactician with no desire to strut the shiny boards or to lead the arty life whatsoever—we were able to cook up a plan to help break ourselves in.

As I've already said, both Ian and I come from musical backgrounds. One of the first things you do on starting up a new band—having gathered together the nearest available musicians (the one with the van, the one who can write and the one whose dad won't mind you rehearsing in his garage); agreed upon a name (through a combination of straw poll and drunken fist fight) and established the musical style that you intend to milk (because it's the only thing that your drummer can play)—is to find yourself a 'look'. Few musicians join bands in the hope of becoming international rock superstars. They do it because it gives them a legitimate excuse to dress up, wear big boots and put makeup on. Mainstream poets don't tend to do that so much, (well, not out in the open, anyway) which I'd always felt was something of a wasted opportunity. It's all about 'veracity and virtue' with that lot, the baring of the soul, stripping it all back to the fundamental and 'tellin' it like it is'. There are dozens of beardy-bloke poets in checked shirts, jeans and sensible shoes out there, almost as many as there are singer/songwriters who also look like they've spent the morning teaching maths and didn't have time to get changed before hitting the O2 Stage. Alright, granted, it should be more about the content than the casual transvestitism: the material should always come first, but if

10

it's work that you're looking for or the chance of being remembered for being something that little bit different, then it can't hurt the brand to be distinguishable in a crowd as well, can it? Maybe I'm missing something, but that's my philosophy, anyway.

The 'Look' that we arrived at (and probably the reason why people stick with us at a music or comedy event, when they would ordinarily have buggered off the moment they heard that there was a poet on next) has been variously described as 'goth', 'steampunk', 'tranny-lite' or just plain 'unnecessary'. Poet Laura Dockrel, backstage in Norwich in 2010, remarked that it was 'like sharing a dressing room with a rock band'. That was probably because we were hogging the mirror and choking her with hairspray.

But it isn't a contrived look, this, as many have speculated, we didn't sit down with Vivienne Westwood one afternoon with the intention of designing something that would turn heads and make people want to stick around for long enough to let us get a piece out, no; it just happened. We're a couple of old tarts by nature who can't actually see why you shouldn't market poetry or comedy (or any other form of entertainment) with the same showbiz pizazz that you would a band. I have a particular penchant for black PVC and bondage wear: I always have done; I've tried therapy, but it didn't work. Ian has a thing for leather'n lace and…tights and we both like big boots and tattoos and Donna, well, she saw us as 'ironic Byronic'. We already had most of this shit in our wardrobes long before we ever put words to riff and, anyway, who really gives a lovelorn sonnet what people think of the way we choose to look? If they're thinking about it enough to pass comment, though, then surely we've made our point!

Point two on the plan: get a gig somewhere. Anywhere.

Now, there is a tried and tested route to poetry circuit acceptance. There is a well-beaten path and an etiquette to be observed if one wants to be welcomed into the community and to be taken seriously as a jobbing bard. For Dawkins' sake don't go in all guns a'blazin', especially if your poetic stylings are in the least bit left of field. You must show

11

deference aplenty to the 'Bards Of...', 'The Laureates Of...' and the 'Slam Winners Of...' if you're ever going to make a mark in this pretentious little cultural bubble.

The 'scene' are very keen on their titles and their awards. In an art form where so many individuals choose to adopt such shamelessly derivative styles of delivery, it is perhaps inevitable that they'll rely quite heavily on yardsticks to point out 'who da' best'.

Donna's background is competitive sports. She would have thoroughly enjoyed the whole slam poetry route. Ian would not have been averse to a spot of competitive arts either; he loves nothing greater than watching fast cars driving round in a circle on a Sunday afternoon, but it's one of my 'things', y'see. I don't do competition; never have done. I can appreciate its momentary merit for testing two athletes of the same discipline, to see who's fastest the day, but try as I have, I cannot see the relevance of competition if the competitors are not attempting to do exactly the same thing at the same time.

'Oh, you're just scared of losing,' has often been levelled at me by poetry champions and titled tosspots of the trade. Think what you like, yon bards of bugger all: you can't make me do it! Everyone has the right to express themselves artistically without having to compete for the privilege.

Refusal, though, does make life as a performance poet newcomer a little difficult.

So we decided to set up our own showcasing gig, specializing in the weird and the wonderful: other acts who were having the same trouble we were, fitting into recognisable boxes and who might compliment us. Cue the re-draughting of Philfy Phil, Poeterry and The Artwist, who at that point had been faring no better than ourselves in the big wide world beyond open mic.

And so RRRANTS was born; 'Rhythmical Ravings & Rants', to be precise; a loose collective of offbeat performance artistes and general audience-stalking weirdos in search of a kicking off point. As a two-fingered salute to the circuit that we were about to attempt to circumvent, we held our first four events in The Poetry Society's very own basement The Poetry Cafe in Betterton Street, Covent Garden. We had intended to promote four shows per year there, offering performance spots to newcomers, along with (just as importantly) more established performers (who also ran their own nights) and who were eager to use our shows as a convenient place to hand out flyers. Within a year, our original four would become more than a hundred oddball performers from all over the country, gigging with us on a regular basis. We soon found ourselves with a lot of new friends, along with invites to perform at the more bohemian of the already well established poetry, comedy and cabaret events up and down the country. Within a couple of years we were running five nights per MONTH—so much for four a year—in a number of venues in London and the Home Counties and attracting some of the bigger names in poetry, music and comedy as headline to our ubiquitous support.

The plan had worked! A review in *The Stage* newspaper in 2010 was also of great help to us in building up a reputation that might, in time, eclipse the slam titles that people were always expecting of us.

There was a positive plethora of poetry nights opening up all over the country at this time, spewing forth poets whom, just a few years earlier, might never have had the chance to spout their individual ravings.

We were far from being the only act to find this alternative route in and we weren't too proud to jump onto this new-wave train with all four rockbooted feet and to work our arses off whilst the going was good.

2009-2014 was an interesting time to be poeting, especially if you had something unusual to say or an off kilter way of putting whatever it was that you did say across. We were lucky: we hit the ground at exactly the right moment. 'Scenes' come and go in any art form. As of the time of writing this part, (late '15/early '16) the scene that we were able to hitch our ride with is in decline. Many of our contemporaries have moved on. There are still pockets of resistance, but the poeting world is changing once more. New nights are springing up to replace the old; audiences and poets alike are getting younger again; new things are being said and this is as it should be. The next generation are hot on our heels!

The reviews that we received and the contacts that we made were the stepping stones that we'd needed to help us to break out. We gained a lot of experience too, not to mention material as, like the whores that we are, we took every gig that it was possible for us to do, regardless of whether or not we were likely to end up out of pocket in the process. It'd just seemed the obvious thing to do if one wanted to stake a claim. Granted, we weren't trying to make a living out of it: we both had day jobs that paid our general living expenses (cheats, I hear you cry!) and looked upon our poeting lives as a hobby with potential. And we both had cars, unlike a lot of our London-based peers who had to worry about fares and train timetables before saying yes to an engagement. Some of the arse-end-of-nowhere gigs that we've done would've been impossible even to find without a car at one's disposal and I wouldn't have liked to have had to find my way back to civilisation over the top of that mountain pass near Shrewsbury in the dark and on foot!

I've spoken to hundreds of poets over the past few years though, who have lamented the fact that they can't find enough work to make it all pay, then—as a sub clause to that statement—tell me that they can only manage one, or at a push two gigs a week because they get tired. Now, whilst this is by no means most of them, it is a worrying trend.

'Why, after six gigs on the bounce,' we were asked by a fellow poet, whilst packing up on a Sunday morning after a slot at the Larmer Tree Festival, near Shaftsbury, Dorset in 2010, 'would you want to drive for four hours, all the way to Buxton, Derbyshire, to do fifteen unpaid minutes, then drive all the way home again the same night?'

Because we can? Because we might get reviewed? Because it'll be fun? Because we've never been there? Because we might sell CDs? Because we might get spotted and offered something better?

I hadn't wanted to go to Oxford three nights earlier, the fourth gig of that bounce, but I'd gone and we'd received our gold dust review from *The Stage*! In Buxton we met Jo Bell, one of only fourteen audience members that night, who had been given the job of booking new acts for the infamous Ledbury Poetry Festival the following year. Now, if we hadn't gone to Buxton…

It's about putting yourself out there; we'd learnt that from our music days. If it's possible to get there, if it's not going to kill us or bankrupt us in the process, then for Hegley's sake, we do it!

We've had a lot of flack from our contemporaries over the years about the calibre of gig that we've been able to blag without doing things 'properly', as it were: as if we've been 'cheating' somehow. Well I can honestly say that neither of us has ever slept with anyone in order to bag a gig! Nor has Donna. We have never kidnapped anybody's children nor attempted to blackmail anybody with information that we've picked up in the green room or around a campfire at a festival late at night after the alcohol and the anecdotes have been flowing freely. We started out in this industry in the erroneous belief that there were only four performance poets in existence: The aforementioned Attila, plus John Hegley, Jesus Cooper-Clarke and Pam Ayres, none of whom we knew personally, and so the charge of nepotism cannot be levelled at us either! We've got what we've got by saying yes to everything we've ever been offered, by being reliable and by not pricing ourselves out of the market.

'The jewel in Larmer's crown, The Antipoet; the beatrapping duo: this festival's heroes. It's unexpectedly delightful things like this that make Larmer Tree (Festival) what it is.'
—*Bournemouth Echo,* July 2016

Backstage with Tony Pillage 2016 (Donna Ray)

'Bards Of Bugger All' promo shot 2016 (Jonathan Lambton)

16

Backstage at Glastonbury 2016 (Donna Ray)

3. Festivals, I Shit 'Em

"I love these guys—funny, ranty, anarchic, silly and tight as the proverbial gnat's derrière"
—Scott Tyrrell, *Glastonbury Poetry and Words Stage* blogger 2015

If you've bought this book rather than stolen it; and if you HAVE stolen it, then SHAME ON YOU! (Don't you realise that, other than Dr Cooper Clarke, poets earn naff all from gigs and only get to eat dependant on the amount of shit that they can sell afterwards?)

If you HAVE bought it, then that's probably for one of three reasons:

1/ Pity.

2/ It's the only way to obtain all of our better known pieces on a single disc. (Cheapskate!)

3/ You're so fed up with me getting the words wrong every time you come out to see us and you'd really like to know what they are supposed to be about.

You'll probably have brought it at a gig somewhere. Poetry doesn't sell all that well in shops unless it's curriculum based, which this, sadly, isn't and is therefore more commonly flogged 'in the moment', at a live performance, just after the punter has witnessed the act, when they are at their most vulnerable and sympathetic to the poet's whingeful cause. Thank you. It's appreciated. No, really, it is! Hopefully we made you laugh; that was, after all, the plan. People like a laugh, don't they?

Those of you who have been following us around for a while, however, will be aware that we didn't start out as 'a comedy act'. In fact, if you've bought any of our albums or seen us doing more than just a thirty-minute festival stage set, then you'll be aware that we're not just a one-trick pony spouting quasi-offensive, foul-mouthed tirades about anything or anybody who has pissed us off this week. We have a serious side as well, which we're hoping you'll spot if you attempt to use this book as a 'rant-along-an-antipoet' aide.

Our first collection, the long=out-of-print (but still available to download) 'TIGHTS NOT STOCKINGS', features some of our more sober (yet still cynical) musings. This was the direction that we'd expected to follow. I'd thought that we might do the odd funny piece, if I could work out how to write them. It was whilst at The Edinburgh Fringe in August 2009, though, that things took a turn. The Antipoet didn't have a show at The Fringe that year, we were there purely to help publicise a play that I had written and directed. I had paid my actors too well, you see, and had been expecting too much of them (an hour a day is a killer, apparently) and two out of the three of them were refusing to busk or to hand out flyers for the show. So Ian and I cobbled together a set of our funniest poems, used the theatre to rehearse in and then hit The Royal Mile busking stages along with every open mic that we could blag, to do it for them. With so many other performers to challenge and so many oblivious punters just walking past ignoring us, we had to learn to edit and hone our material fast. After that first Edinburgh, the die had been cast, though. People began to see us as 'comedy' and our direction changed a tad. Those of you who have bought our albums will know that, although we tend to err toward the funnier material live, we do still like to add a few of the more temperate pieces to our discs to shake things up a bit and to remind people that we are poets and not just a comic turn.

But what does it really matter? Our roots are poetic; most defiantly, as you'll know if you've been reading this from the front rather than just dipping in to read the poems. But should we care how people describe us, should we pander to the arrogant designations that we are assigned? Should any of us care whether we fit into a pre-prescribed box or not? Should any artist, for that matter, be asking themselves if that new piece that they've just given long and arduous birth to, fits neatly within the tightly delineated parameters of what the pedant police will regard as the very definition of their chosen genre?

Do you like what you're seeing/hearing/tasting/fondling or shoving up your arse or not? Because that's all that matters really.

...unless, of course, one is looking to make a career out of what one does.

'What's your goal?' we were asked in an interview recently, 'ultimately, obviously, where do you see yourselves going with this act?'

Now, I'm not usually flummoxed in radio interviews—I'm the one they're usually making 'wind it up' hand gestures at to get me to shut up so they can play a Lionel Ritchie record—but this question threw us both. We'd no idea. Weirder acts than us have gone on to international TV, radio, film and stadium success, but it's not something that we've ever seriously expected to need to consider.

'Where do you expect to see yourselves in five years time?' he went on, presuming us to have not quite understood his line of questioning the first time around.

To be honest, I don't think either of us had ever expected to have done the things that we have done!

'You'll never do Ledbury,' we were told, by people who knew such things and who didn't want us to lower the tone of the country's most prestigious poetry festival; 'Don't even bother applying to Glastonbury,' we were told, by people who had themselves been submitting without luck for several years.

'They'll never book you for a Royal Variety Performance, you know,' said Donna and she knows about these things (she did, however, manage to negotiate us the first two of those, so maybe we should have pushed her for the third!

As I've already said, making a living out of poetry—and when I say a living, I mean being able to pay my mortgage, run my car and be able to keep my goat and chickens in the manner to which they have become accustomed (and in Ian's case, being able to satiate his twin passions of 'kit acquisition' and silk lingerie procurement)—isn't as easy as it would seem to be for performers in some other mediums. Yes, we'd love to do this full time! How much fun would that be? I'd love a job that didn't actually entail doing any work, but neither of us is prepared to take the pay cut that would involve. Does that mean that we're not serious about what we do? No. We just can't envisage a future where what we do covers all that.

Oh, you CAN make a good living from poetry; yes I know and many people do, but rarely doing it quite the way that we do. A lot of poets go the schools route: peripatetically speakin' out t'd'yout. We've done two schools in our time. The first didn't ask us back— probably because I upset a couple of the kids—and the second asked us to leave, which was a blessing as the little bastards were about to turn ugly!

Schools, then, it would seem, are probably not for us.

You rarely see a professional poet making decent money anywhere else, though. You may hear the voices of the likes of Roger McGough and the ever pervasive JCC on adverts or Pam Ayres outlasting the comics on 'Just A Minute', but what else is there for us? (Mind you, I'd be happy with any of that!) Craig Charles crossed over into acting, I suppose, and Phil (Porky The Poet) Jupitus is a shining beacon of hope to all of us, but that's still barely a handful.

Comedians, on the other hand, have plenty of opportunities to upscale. They can kick off with a spot on a radio 4 panel show or a news based quiz, if they have a tenacious enough agent at their back, then work their way onto the televisual version of the show where they can be appreciated by a wider, younger demographic. If they're lucky, Dave TV will then contrive a six-part vehicle to showcase their particular talents or maybe some form of fact finding travelogue if they can't think of anything else to put them in. If, after this, people are still laughing, then they might get a guest spot on 'Live At The Apollo', leading to another on 'Loose Women', before going on to either host their own game show or, if they're really lucky, get their own sitcom! Storm that and well, you could find yourself starring in a remake of the film that broke the last British comic to attract Hollywood! But poets?

No one knows quite what to do with them, do they? As musicians we had an ambition; admittedly, it was the same ambition that drives every other musician: an ambition that needs no explanation here, but would ultimately take one on to the same place that the comedian went.

So where do we see ourselves in five years time? What giddy heights are we planning to conquer in the name of all those who'll come after us? Well, in Ian's case, he'd like to be seen playing on Jools Holland's television show.

For me, I'm aiming at being cast as Doctor Who. Any more stupid questions, Mr DJ?

The turning point in our fortunes really came with the offer of a slot at The Larmer Tree Festival in 2010. We'd never done a festival before that. Up until that point, playing at a proper festival had been Ian's main ambition in life. We'd done a lot of pubs and arts centres, the odd teashop and The Northampton Labour Club, but nothing on quite such a scale. The chance came about when we were turned down for Glastonbury. 'They won't even look at your application,' miffed applicants past had told us, 'don't waste your time. It's a closed shop.'

Well, it isn't; that's just bollocks. Alright, you may not get chosen the first or even the second time you apply or even ever (especially with that attitude), but they receive thousands of applications every year from all over the world; poets who are prepared to pay their own airfare from half way round the world. Your application needs to look shit hot!

So, when we weren't chosen, instead of firing off a bitter and self-pitying electronic tirade at the nice lady who runs the stage, (many a poet's instant indignant inclination) Donna sent her a contrite line to thank her for considering us and to say that, in the unlikely event that anybody might cancel at short notice, we would not be too proud to be considered last minute replacements. Now, I'm not suggesting that was what won her over, but politeness, my mother taught me, won't harm your cause. Within a week we had been offered a replacement slot at The Larmer Tree Festival on the poetry stage run by said same promoter, the very lovely, Helen Johnson. We were on our best behaviour all weekend, keen to show that not only could we handle the pressure of a big festival stage, but that we were reliable, and easy to deal with.

We're both glad that we did Larmer Tree before being chosen for Glastonbury. We may have felt ready for the big one in 2010, but in retrospect, we really weren't and luckily it would be another year of working up to it before we'd receive the offer.

Whereas Ian was ecstatic to be on the festival 'scene', I have to say, it really wasn't me. Call me a snob; call me a wimp, but I'd vowed when I'd left the Boy's Brigade, never to do tents or chemical Khazees again! So there we were at our first festival with Ian in a tent with all the relevant accoutrements for a six-month trek across the pole and Donna and myself in a nice little B+B, five miles up the road. Extravagant, we know, but at this point, we really weren't expecting to be doing this kind of thing all that often, so had chosen to indulge in a bit of luxury.

With our first festival stage duly chalked up, Donna and I headed back to the B+B for a warm bath, but Ian had other ideas. He was off the leash for the night and at a proper outdoor music fest and he had a backstage pass and everything!

He enjoyed himself. There was some mention of a flexible young dancer, a tent pole and a bottle of Southern Comfort and the next thing he knew, he was scrabbling around to try to locate his phone to hear me giving him the news that we'd just been offered a last minute replacement spot at the Buxton Fringe; a mere four hours' drive away and we could make it if we left now! Neither of us can quite recall his full hungover response, but it involved the words, 'We're Artists!' and a new poem was born.

Glastonbury was quite the game changer for us.

We saw it as a validatory move: here was our chance to show 'The Inner Clique' just what we could do! Here was our chance to make some friends amongst 'em, now that we were 'officially' a part of the 'scene', as it were, not to mention some useful contacts!

We'd never really been that worried about being a part of anything

23

before, but here it was being offered and, well… we were as enchanted as a pair of kittens with a loose piece of thread.

We were being entrusted with our biggest gig to date and we weren't about to fuck it up. Ian was beside himself. I, however, was horrified! On the one hand, 'this was it!' It didn't get any better, but on the other hand, I'd never had the slightest desire to go anywhere like that! I was terrified. Festivals just weren't my bag; they never had been.

Oh, I'd done a few by that point, but nothing on that scale and more importantly: not one where I had to stay over. I told you: I DON'T DO TENTS AND CHEMICAL KHAZEES!

So, we hired a camper van, which for that week each June is no mean feat. No respectable van hire specialist sends their assets to Glastonbury, so we got ours from 'Shonky Sid', someone that an ex-girlfriend of Ian's had once met at a party. It was expensive, but we were desperate and grateful, so bloody grateful: anything rather than sleeping on the floor. We loaded it up with every bit of kit we'd ever worn (just in case, you understand) and set a course for Pilton, Somerset.

'Don't take it over fifty', the owner, who hadn't bothered to clean it out before charging us way over the odds for his rusty, mildew-stained chicken coop on wheels had said, 'it's got a new engine.'

'New', you say?

Well, to say that it struggled would be to presume it'd actually been trying. This was not a happy van. I'm sure it'd begged its owner to allow it to rust away with dignity in a field some years before, but it was not to be that lucky and neither were we, as it died it's final, protracted death just shy of Andover, on the A303 to Salisbury.

So often over the years have I guiltily offered up an atheist's hypocritical prayer as I've loaded my suitcases into the car on the morning of a holiday:

'Please, car, just get me to the airport, I beg of thee. I'll send you for a full service the moment I get back. I don't care if you break down when we get there; I can always phone the RAC to tow us home.'

Or: 'Please, people who run the M25, don't be playing that damnable "variable speed limit" game today. I know it must be a lot of fun for you, sitting in your office, watching the chaos mount up on your camera feeds, but I really need to catch this plane...'

For what worse a time could there be to break down?

'It's okay,' I told Ian, 'the RAC will tow us there.'

Hmmm. Read the small print, boy. They will tow you to either your planned destination or back home: whichever's CLOSEST, and we were about ten miles shy of being halfway to Glastonbury.

It cost us three CDs, but 'Frank' (not his real name; I've changed it so as not to get him into trouble) eventually agreed to load us up and take us to the festival.

'No idea how you'll get home, though,' he reassured us, as he unloaded us backstage at "Theatre & Circus", 'you can only be recovered once, y'know.'

Did we care? We were at Glastonbury! Nothing else mattered.

We were late, but we didn't miss the first of our two slots of the weekend. Did I say two? No sooner had we been deposited from the back of Frank's truck, but I was receiving a text from Dennis-Just-Dennis: a poet whom we'd had on our stage in Camden a couple of years before.

'Just seen your name in the programme,' he said, 'do you fancy a gig at The Fluffy Rock Cafe, tomorrow lunchtime?'

Don't mind if we do!

It was Dennis who took us under his wing and showed us around the festival, introducing us to the various bar and cafe proprietors who were happy to stand our food and drink bills if we would give them a thirty minute set at our very convenience. We played eight times that weekend, but we paid for absolutely nothing.

And we did make some friends, though not the ones we'd expected. Through playing the many bars and cafes that year, we met a number of people from other festivals, who snapped us up for the following year. We also got speaking to some of the stage managers for Glastonbury's 'lesser known' stages, with a view to finding an 'in' if our debut on the "Poetry & Words" were to prove less than enthralling.

But pull it off we did and we seemed to go down well; well, we must've done, as we got asked back for a second year!

Cue another of those pure luck "right time, right place" career enhancing nexus points, as the mysterious body who put together the annual Glastonbury programme—the printed, £15 a copy, glossy listings magazine of artists to watch and events not to miss—decided that year (2014) to run a feature of things that you may not have realised you needed to see. At number eight in their fortuitous countdown was the aforementioned "Poetry & Words" stage and, just by chance, they chose a picture of The Antipoet to illustrate their point. A big picture. A full page picture. Somewhere in the region of half a million people spend a weekend at Worthy Farm each June, sampling the delights, legal and not, of the world's most famous arts festival, each of whom would have seen that picture of him'n me in all our A4 monochrome glory. We could never have afforded that level of publicity without a record company's backing and yet there it was for free! We played fifteen slots that year, revisiting stages we'd played before and finding a few more besides.

If you haven't been to Glastonbury, then take it from us: it's much, much bigger than the BBC would have you believe. Counting all the smaller stages, there are something like eighty platforms over a seven-mile circumference pumping out all manner of entertainment from midday 'til six am for three consecutive days. It's vast! What are the chances, then, that we'll be walking behind a gaggle of girls on the Saturday afternoon and overhear this snippet of conversation:

'The Stones aint on 'til nine, 'Shell; what we gunna do 'til then?'

'Well I was finkin', right, we might take in some cultcha an' go'n watch them An'ipoets; wha' d'you reckon?'

… NOUS AVON ARRIVÉ!

From 2015 we took over the Poetry & Words 'warm up' spot, the slot that no-one else wants, first act of the day when everyone's still asleep, but we love it! It means we get to play every day and we get a sound check into the bargain. We've also got the rest of the day free to play the likes of "The Mavericks" late night cabaret stage, The Greenpeace Stage, The Tipi Stage, The Tree (it's in a tree), Fluffy Rock Cafe, The Banjo Stage, so called because it's shaped like a... and a whole host of others spots.

"It was lovely to corrupt the festival with you"
—Helen Johnson, Poetry and Words, Glastonbury June 2014

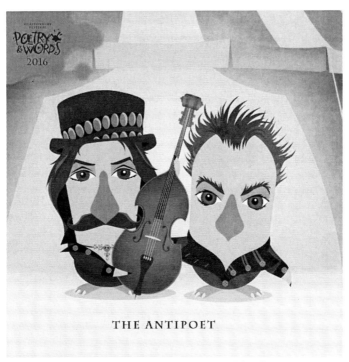

Glastonbury publicity 2016 (Scott Tyrrell)

Glastonbury Poetry and Words 2016 (Donna Ray)

Edinburgh Festival 2015 (Donna Ray)

4. The Albums

"Oh to be a virgin where exposure to The Antipoet is concerned. Chuffing hilarious!"
Dave Quayle, Lillabullero, April 2017

2010 was also the year that we put together our first audio collection: *Tights Not Stockings*. At the time I think we both thought we were being a bit presumptuous. Poets do books; after all, it's about the words, isn't it? But it isn't. I've bought racks of poetry books over the years because I've enjoyed a poet's work, only to get it home and find that it doesn't read quite as well in my voice as it sounded in its author's. Poetry is a bit like a painting in that respect: it's not just what you see that counts, it's as much about what you don't. When you read the annotated works of a comedian, you'll probably only laugh half as much as you would've done had you seen that skit performed. It's the missing rhythms, y'see, the beats, the facial expressions and the pauses that are equally as important as the text on the page.

We took the project to an old friend of mine, drummer and producer Mark Gordon: a man whom I have worked with and trusted for three decades and who knows exactly how to make the most out of any idea you could throw at him.

It was Mark's suggestion that we add percussion and effects to the tracks. We have only very rarely done this live, but after hearing his first mix, we all three agreed with him that the recorded, definitive versions needed to sound more substantial than their live counterparts. There were those who disagreed, however, countering that we are what we are and that that is what people want to take home with them after they've seen us live. Perhaps we were being too ambitious with our glossy cover and our poetry CD marketed to look and sound like a rock album?

In two minds, for our second collection in 2011, (*Hanging With Poets*) we scaled everything down and recorded ten new tracks with just the original bass and vocals and we did it in my garage. It should have been easy. We even released it in a 'throw-away' PVC plastic wallet rather than the jewel case and wrap around cover that we'd plumped for on the initial pressing of *Tights...*, but the problem, as with all 'do-it-yourself' recordings, is that you need that third ear: an independent opinion to tell you when you're being self-indulgent. We took it to another old friend and musical collaborator, Beef Grant, who got Ian to re-record the bass and backing vocals and then remixed it for us. The first two pressings of the album were exactly that, but comparisons began to be made with the glossier first disc and so, just shy of embarking on our third album, we gave Mark the master of number two and got him to pimp it up. There are two distinctly different versions of this disc out there in the world, the most common being the later, 'Flash Mix' version with added percussion. It's the standard that we have gone with for each disc since.

Whilst we are on the subject of album trivia, if you have a copy of the original pressing *Tights...* in its aforementioned cracked jewel case, with its paper label (which peels off inside your CD player when it gets warm) and the fold out cover featuring a line-up of bestockinged legs, we can now reveal that only TWO of those pairs of silky, shapely pins belong to bonafide girls (and I doubt it's the pair you'd expect!). The fish-netted legs on the label, however, are real and belong to Donna!

It wasn't until we were preparing to record our third album, in early 2012, that we began to feel that we finally had a handle on what it was that we actually did. *Random Words* was our most confident collection of those first three, not to mention the only one of that set that we'd written with the intention of it being an actual collection. We'd stopped agonising over whether what we were producing fell into which particular camp, by that point. Let them make of it what they will, we'd decided; what did it matter as long as people were prepared to book us and to buy the bloody CDs? And they were!

31

Personally, I think it's probably our most cynical album to date. Buoyed by the fact that we seemed to have gained a somewhat unwarranted reputation as 'foul-mouthed poetry yobs', I think, in retrospect, we must have taken the unconscious decision to play to the gallery a tad on this one. Donna had been approached on several separate occasions by promoters wanting to book us, but who had asked her if it would be at all possible for us to keep the coarse language to a minimum. Up until that point, there had barely been a cuss or a curse in any of our most regularly thumbed pieces and certainly nothing offensive enough to have caused walkouts, like some circuit contemporaries I could mention! (In fact the only walkouts that I can ever recall were the winner of a poetry prize and his mother, at a charity run prize-giving event in Beaconsfield in '09. We'd been booked as the turn, but the disgruntled parent felt that we weren't 'real poets' and made a very loud exit and then there was that elderly gentleman at the Ledbury festival in '10 who shuffled out on account of the battery dying in his hearing aid!)

Random Words In A Random Order, with its punk rock stylings: two angry blokes, black-nailed fingers in salute and its 'parental advisory' label, imbued us with the yobbie credentials that were so expected of us. Even so, it's no *Derek and Clive—Ad Nauseum* nor *Never Mind The Bollocks here's The Sex Pistols*. It's a rant, yes; guilty as charged, officer. It's sarcastic, anarchic, it's trying very hard to be subversive, but it's also got its serious side.

As much as its title track is about the pretentious guff spouted by many a pompous 'right on' poet, who's chosen to believe his or her own hype, it's also about us taking the rise out of our own unearned and misconstrued repute; with its repetitively vernacular chorus of 'what the fuck?' and its apparent mindless rant against our poeting peers. That's the thing about poetry: unlike a gag, it's written to be read and re-read; its true meaning often only being revealed with study. (Jesus, now I'm sounding as masturbatory as the archetypes we were attempting to expose!)

The punters, it seemed, got it straightaway though, and without it having to be explained to them, but many of our fellow poets took exception to our breaking of the fourth wall, as it were. Apparently, they could see themselves in our ire and felt that we were taking cheap and unprovoked potshots at them and at 'the art' that they represented. Well, we were, a bit, but none of those who'd seen the piece as a personal affront were actually correct in their targeting assumptions. IT ISN'T ABOUT ANYBODY IN PARTICULAR! IT'S MERELY AN OBSERVATION and one that so many punters agreed with. Stop taking yourselves so seriously! You'll enjoy life so much more if you just relax. Yes, it's true that I did start to write it whilst waiting our turn at a particularly dull and overly worthy poetry night in a South London pub (and if you were there that night, then I can see how you may have thought I was aiming it at you), but I could equally have written it anywhere else that we'd played that year!

In the March of 2012, we were approached by poetry champions 'Bang Said The Gun'—contemporaries of ours on the London poetry promotion circuit, though with far more panache and influence than RRRANTS, (our own promotional arm) would ever muster—to provide the theme music to a television pilot that they were making for SKY TV. They wanted 'Random Words' to be at the beginning of each episode of a potential new stand-up poetry series. This was the first time that I'd actually seen a real possibility for us, beyond entertaining ourselves and our friends, of course. If any of our poeting cohorts could bring this underground scene to the fore then it was Dan, Martin and Rob of Bang!

Sadly, the recording wasn't a great experience for us. We weren't universally liked by our peers anyway and if any of our pieces was guaranteed to divide an audience, then it was 'Random Words'. The whole evening felt awkward and uncomfortable and ultimately, when the pilot was cut for broadcast, our contribution didn't make it out of

33

the editing suite.

There was to be a protracted gap before the recording of the next album. Read any biography of a well-known media double act and you'll find a point where those two individuals weather a troublesome patch in their professional partnership. When two good friends begin working together, cracks in their personal relationships often start to appear. It's often blamed on the pressure of work: the long hours, late nights, the royalty splits or 'irreconcilable differences', (which is where one half of a duo starts receiving more attention than the other). None of that was ever likely to become a problem for us, though, as neither were we famous, ever likely to become so, or... friends. We'd started out as 'associates', we worked well together, but we had bugger all in common, bar the fact that, for the purpose of what we were trying to achieve, what one of us lacked, the other possessed: namely I'm not a competent musician and Ian's not a poet. We needed each other to make this idea work, which was equally frustrating for both of us, as neither of us would otherwise have spent quite that amount of time in the other's company.

For the most part it worked, though. Yes we wind each other up occasionally: I'm an awkward, moody bastard (or 'artist' as I prefer to be described) and he has a self-destructive side to his nature which tended to manifest itself in his choice of girlfriend, though he latterly seems to have solved that problem, but we'd made it work thus far.

Let me be the first to say that I can be a right git to work with. I'm stubborn, controlling, impatient and easily bored, (though let me also take this opportunity to dispel that much bandied rumour that I routinely steal both the credit and the reward for other people's work. I have never, nor would ever do this, but unfortunately, not everyone in this industry understands the way that The Performing Rights system works!)

It's the creating that drives me, more than it is the performing; in stark opposition to The Bass Whore, who didn't earn that moniker without good reason! We would be doing two new sets a year if it was down to me. Ian, on the other hand, is keener to keep improving upon what we have. We meet somewhere in the middle, or at least we learnt to do so, during our 'soul searching' year of '13. Being forced to share a broken-down, mould-riddled camper van for four days at Glastonbury festival helped to clear the air as well!

Ere's One For The Kiddies was to be two years in the making.

In retrospect, that was probably for the better, if for no other reason than we were able to fulfil an ambition of mine to include a 'Live At Glastonbury...' track as an extra on the album.

It had a trixy birth, this one, and there were times during its delivery where we were both wondering whether we'd taken this 'open mic rebellion' thing as far as it could go. We were gigging damn near nightly. Our mates had stopped coming along, presumably because they were as bored of hearing the same old shizzle as I was of performing it.

Ian was in demand playing in his many bands, all of which paid far more than an Antipoet appearance was ever likely to, and I, unlike with everything else that I was doing at the time, just could not see where this weird act could possibly take us. There didn't seem to be any precedent.

One part of it that I was particularly enjoying, though, was hearing other performers parodying our work. I hadn't seen anyone of our lowly stature complimented in this way before. Donna has always said that at some point we'll do an album that we don't even feature on, full of other poets' piss takes and riffs on our stuff. Fay Roberts was the first, and her version of 'I Like Girls' has now become integral to the original. Comedy songwriter and parodist extraordinaire Philfy Phil quickly followed suit, even recording 'They're Smarties', his version of 'We're Artists', on his own album, (guest starring Ian himself). There was Justin Thyme's 'I like dogs' and the man who has ridiculed us more than anyone, with numerous clever, witty and flattering parodies, ex Bard of Stony Stratford, Richard Frost. Our name has cropped up in several other writers' work too, including that of Stephen Hobbs,

35

Vanessa Horton, Simon David, Poeterry and Nathan Jones, to name only the ones I've heard recently. This more than anything else is what made me realise that what we were doing had a future.

*Kiddies…*was a lot lighter in tone than its immediate predecessor. This wasn't deliberate, it was just the way that it came out. Once again, Mark came up trumps with the editing and mixing and the anime style cover, by our friend Jammie Sammy, also helped to make the album look a little cheekier. I was listening to it again as I was writing this and I'd actually forgotten some of the tracks that we don't perform that often. Most of the gigs that we get booked for are relatively short and need to be hard hitting and (as is usually expected) funny, so we rarely get to do some of the slower, more intense pieces like 'Reading Dogs', 'Tipping Point', '1420Mhz', 'Distraction', 'Members Only' etc.

(Note to self: must do something about that!)

*Kiddies…*is the disc that has so far had the most airplay. We were invited to play a few tracks live for FUBAR Radio: the no-holds-barred comedy station, just after release. We had a great time, as usual, and on our way out, were asked by the producer if we'd like to come back on the weekend, as they were doing a seventy-two-hour, non-stop comedy broadcast. Comedian Mark Watson, (whose 'introducing…' show we'd performed at whilst at The Edinburgh Fringe in '11), was doing one of his famous comedy marathons at The Pleasance Theatre next door and several of his guests were popping in after their spots with him. When we arrived the two presenters had been on air for so long that they were beginning to hallucinate. We set up, were introduced, began our first piece and then noticed our hosts disappearing out of the studio for a break.

'Just keep going,' they said, 'we'll be back in a bit.'

I think we'd played the whole album plus a mix of 'past faves' before they reappeared.

Bards Of Bugger All ranks as my all-time favourite recording experience to date. I've never felt at home in a recording studio and I've probably

36

spent years of my life in them: they're confined and artistically stifling. Conversely, Ian would happily spend all day in one, overdubbing, retaking and sculpting the perfect performance. This session, however, was a dream.

Again it'd taken us two years to get back into the studio, but it was worth the wait on several fronts. For one thing, the track listing that we finished up with was very different from the one that we'd started with. We had twice as many new pieces to choose from this time than we'd actually needed to record plus the time, due to several cancelled recording dates, to hone a coherent and tight collection out of them. More importantly, though, over the course of the time that we'd spent writing and rehearsing the new material, Ian and I actually became mates.

2015 was a much better year for us. We got on better at the festivals, we talked more and we had fun with what we were doing.

In the January of '15, Ian had made a fundamental life change. He'd ditched the 'troublesome' girlfriends and for the first time in his life started living on his own. He'd also finally confessed to those of us around him that he was a transvestite. He had expected us all to be shocked, but we weren't. For the first time since Donna and I had known him he seemed to be at peace with himself, all of his pent up frustration having evaporated overnight. He was a different person (on Tuesdays'n Thursdays). He laughed more. We all laughed more. He was far more fun to be around, (though I wish he'd learn to keep his legs together when we're rehearsing!)

Since we first realised that there was comic potential to be had from this act, Ian has been the unwitting stooge to many a cruel and caustic on-stage remark of mine. For the most part his response has been just to camp it up, occasionally firing off the odd sharp and witty retort in reply, but usually just lapping up the audience's sympathy, like many a 'Buttons' has to a panto 'Abenazzer'. Sometimes my adlib, spur of the moment jibes have gone too far, though, but whereas the old Ian might have thought I was being a git, the new improved Ian can take a joke

37

the way it's meant and give back as good (if not better) than he gets!

The night before the recording, we got together in my back room for a sensible final run through of the set. That's what should've happened. What actually happened was that we got pissed and decided to write a whole new piece for the album from scratch, based on my wry observations of how he could be a better tranny. We probably should've left it there—it was, after all, shit, (funny, but shit)—but we decided instead to record it anyway. So having laid down the first ten tracks, we left the tape running and just went for it. Again, we probably should've left it there, but the resulting cacophony of bum notes, missed cues, mangled lyrics and unlikely harmonies seemed to sum up the change in our working relationship over the past year so perfectly that we left it all in to show anybody who cared that we'd really had a great afternoon and were enjoying working together. It's called 'Do The Tranny Shuffle', and, though it isn't listed on the sleeve notes, if you leave your disc running after the end of the live tracks, you'll find it about a minute in.

'So, what are you s'posed to be?' asks the small child, as we step from the stage at the 'Small World' Festival in Kent in August '16, having just played an hour's 'poetry' set to an audience of tie-dyed wizards, chainsaw wielding 'artists', breast feeding mothers and random naked people.

'What am I supposed to be?'

This is a proper festival: one where a girl can collapse in front of the stage after imbibing a cocktail of sun, smoke and 'special blend tea' and be encouraged to stop fitting by friends who 'just want to see the band, man'; a place where a man in six-inch tranny boots and fishnet stockings needs to be careful of taking a menu at face value (Ian!) and where the kids are making more sense than their parents.

It's been asked before this question, numerous times and by many and varied a punter, presenter or poetical impresario, though never, I have to say, by someone quite so earnest in their artless bewilderment.

Our answer, though, has always been the same:

'We're poets, my dear: Poetry is what we do. Is it not blindingly obvious?'

'But where are you GOING with it?' the child's mother slurrily interjects, detaching her latest offspring and putting it down to play with the campfire, rearranging her hessian blouse as she attempts to focus on my faces.

'We're going as far as poets can reasonably be expected TO go,' I reply, tiredly, but firmly; like a Tory MP on the campaign trail, dejectedly explaining his party's stance on the three-class system to the umpteenth doorstepped pleb of the day.

'Poets, that is,' I continue, firmly, trying not to sound too despondent, 'who don't play the schools circuit and who refuse, as a matter of principle, to compete with other poets.'

These had been our standard answers to those oft asked questions for the past eight years.

But where DO poets go: what exactly is at the top of that particular metaphorical tree and just what was it that we were trying to achieve here?

We didn't really know. Truth be told, we'd never really known; in lieu of a wealth of similarly minded, sonnet-conscious role models to emulate, we'd simply just repeated that same, time-worn mantra in the hope that a proper answer might one day become apparent in a 'burning bush to a wandering prophet' kind of way. We'd still been repeating it as we'd set out on this, our 'Bards Of Bugger All' tour in the March of that year (our most ambitious and pompous undertaking to that point) and we'd been repeating it throughout said tour, but at some point along the way, we'd finally begun to see things differently…

We'd started the tour at a poetry gig in Soho, London: guests on a poetry bill, as we had been so many times before, performing with our peers on that circuit and to an audience that viewed us as 'poets', mainly because the evening had been advertised thusly and so poetry was what one would have expected. We gave them our show and nobody complained; well, not that we're aware of, anyway. Certainly nobody stood up and shouted: 'Gadzooks! Have a care: that's not what I call proper poetry, dear boy!' in a theatrically fruity accent, whilst waving a dipped quill and declaiming his effrontery a haiku.

We ended the tour, however, six months later, billed as a 'band' at a music festival in Derby.

We played the same set for both gigs and in exactly the same way. Between the March and the September we'd played at a variety of different festivals, events and gigs, sometimes billed as poets, occasionally listed as 'comedy', quite often as 'cabaret' and once, at Camp Bestival in Dorset in the July, as 'kids' entertainment.

Same act, same set, and often to people who'd been to more than one show and were happy enough to buy our CDs regardless of which particular artistic bracket we fell into.

It was on the journey back from Camp Bestival that we had our Damascene moment, suddenly and binaurally coming to the conclusion that it really didn't matter how we were billed just as long as we WERE billed. Not that long before that, whilst working on new material, Ian had chided me for making our 'chori' too melodic.

'Speak it, don't sing it!' he'd so often berated, 'it's supposed to be poetry.'

But did it really matter how we, or indeed, anybody else, chose to label what we do? Do you like it; do you get it; did it make you laugh? What more do we need to know?

We'd arrived in Lulworth Cove for the Camp Bestival gig expecting to be playing on the poetry stage as nobody had told us otherwise. We obviously hadn't read the small print because, on arrival, we were directed to the 'kids' field' ("left at the helterskelter, mate; just past The Clangers") and to a tent filled with under-fives.

'You've got a kids' set, haven't you?' asked the promoter, when we protested that we might have been misbooked. He'd seen us playing at a

40

Cambridge fundraiser a few months earlier, a little over lubricated and foul-mouthed as a result, and he'd booked us on the spot!

'No,' we replied in unison.

'Oh, you'll be fine,' he assured us. 'Just try not to swear. The kids'll love you.'

Stepping out into the melee of the kids' field, ten minutes before we were due to go on, in order to thrash out some kind of a game plan for the nightmare that was to come, we ran into a group of child-free people who were busy photographing themselves next to a pair of giant inflatable Clangers.

We got talking (to the people not the Clangers), who were intrigued by our attire (gimp mask included) and we invited them in to witness our impending reputational suicide. It's always better to play to someone rather than no one, we'd reasoned and as 'DJ Death' had just cleared the tent, putting a whole new spin on the term: "death warmed up", we were anxious to create some kind of an adult audience to die to.

But something strange was about to happen. Within ten minutes we'd filled the place with children and parents alike. Not only did they show up, but they apparently loved us, forming an orderly queue to buy our discs and acquire our autographs afterwards! I was even asked by one parent if we did kids' parties!

The randoms whom we'd met by the Clangers seemed to like us too; it later transpired, that one of them was an official reviewer, who listed us as his fourth favourite act of the entire festival, one place above KT Tunstall (Bananarama and Tears For Fears not even featuring in his top five)!

But that's how it works, isn't it? You can toil your arse off in this life playing back-end-of-nowhere youth hostel gigs and old people's homes and still achieve fuck all. It's about being in the right place at the right time when the right person happens to chance past on their way to somewhere else. In the end it all comes down to luck. You put yourself out there (and shit, has she put us out there!), you make sure you're doing as many stages at as many festivals, in as many parts of the country as you possibly can, and if the stars are in the right place that day, if the tea leaves presage it, then you might just be there when that reviewer minces through!

A similar thing had happened to us at 'Larmer Tree Festival' a few weeks before 'Camp Bestival'. We'd taken a busking spot, additional to our pre-arranged stage spots, and got noticed by the reviewer as he headed past us toward the main stage. Those two reviews of 2016 made all the difference for the remainder of the tour. Suddenly more people had heard of us before we arrived at a festival than ever had done before and were ready and waiting to see if we could live up to their expectations. It was a disconcerting feeling for both of us when it first happened, at the 'Green Gathering' in Chepstow, the following week.

We hadn't been expecting the kind of audiences that we were now getting as we toured on through August and September. Of particular interest to us was the fact that no one seeing us for the first time seemed to be the slightest bit troubled by the question of 'what we were'. They'd stopped asking.

So when that young child had asked me what it was that I was supposed to be, I didn't, (as I claimed at the start of this anecdote) roll out my tried'n tested stock answer; neither did I snap at her stoned mother for asking me where we were going with it all. I stopped for a moment, still feeling a little awkward about how we seemed to have started attracting quite a large following of five to ten year olds this season, and I considered my answer.

'What do you think we're supposed to be?' I asked her, turning her innocent query back on her, like the patronising wanker that I must come across as, to anyone of that generation. She looked at me, then she looked at Ian as he stumbled from the tent a little worse for wear, having not given enough consideration to what the fruit in his sangria punch may have been fermenting in. She smiled and she said: 'Funny'. Well, that's good enough for me!

In answer to her maternal role model's inquiry: well, I think I waffled unnecessarily for about twenty minutes. You know, in that poncey, faux existential manner that most artists ramble on in when asked a question about themselves within a few minutes of leaving the stage, whilst the adrenalin is still pumping, and all that. I think I remember laying out our glorious three-year plan in mind numbing detail until she wandered off to sample the punch, wishing she hadn't bothered to ask. I doubt I made a lot of sense: I'd still been riding the high of a gig well received and I don't think I'd quite come down from the rapturous welcome that we'd received at the 'Blythe Power Ashes' in Tewkesbury, the night before (I know Ian hadn't!). I don't really know what I actually said to her, but it certainly wasn't my stock answer of eight years. The truth is, I don't know where we're going with all this and I no longer care.

I'm just enjoying the thrill of the ride!

It's an artist's job to create; if 'job' can be considered a halfway accurate term for what it is that we artists actually do with our time? The moment we stop creating we stagnate and then we lose the right to call ourselves artists at all; well, in my opinion, we do, anyway. Surely creating new work is what it's all about, though, pushing the boundaries that we set for ourselves, trying to find something new to say to the people who bought our previous outpourings and, at the same time, searching for something to inspire new admirers?

There are those who'd disagree, of course. I've met many a creative who was happy to sit back and bask in the glories of successes past rather than create anything new, worried that they might have peaked and that nothing else could ever be as well received as their last offering, but that's up to them. Personally I don't worry about things like that—that way lies paranoia and self-destruction—but then, I enjoy what we do; we both do. We particularly like watching the reactions of punters new to what we do and the faces of regulars hearing something new for the first time. We also get a kick out of people asking us to do pieces that they know from having seen us before, but my biggest thrill is in the writing, imagining how each new line might be received and whether people will laugh where I expect them to or not. If they don't then they don't: we'll write something else. I'm not going to lose any sleep over it. I've spoken to writers who hate the whole writing process, who struggle to give birth to each new piece and who agonise over how their critics might respond to a diversion from their usual tack.

Ian used to fret whenever I told him I had a new idea. He still gets a little anxious when I outline my plans for a new set, but for me it's the whole point of our existence! As I said previously, 'The Antipoet' didn't come about by design; it just happened and, therefore, it has no particular remit. If we want to call ourselves poets, comedians or musicians, this week, then we can. We're not obliged to pay fealty to any distinct format or another; we can do what we bloody well like…

…hence album number six: *We Play For Food*.

For those who haven't heard it, I won't spoil it for you or give you reason not to buy it; suffice to say, we wanted to do something a bit different with this one. Instead of yet another anthology of beat ridden rants, I'd envisaged a collection that flowed from piece to piece in the way that a live gig would. Part of the fun of a live performance is in the adlib 'banter' between ourselves and the audience. Now, we could have just put out a live 'best of' album, including all the usual intros and heckles, but that just seemed too obvious. I wanted to do something that could be considered a show in and of itself. A bit pretentious, you might say, but why not? We're six albums in! If we couldn't do it now, when could we?

To date, though, we've performed it as such just the once, at the album launch night in Stony Stratford, in April '17. We did the whole album, skits'n all, with a specially prepared slide show to illustrate the stories. It was going to be an Edinburgh Fringe show and perhaps it should've been; that'd been the suggestion, but we just couldn't be arsed to go to Edinburgh and do a Fringe show (been there, done it and got the scars to prove it (see my previous book 'THE EDINBURGH FRINGE IN A NUTSHELL, Burning Eye Books 2016 for details)). It could've been a pilot for our Radio 4 show, but the language is a little fruity for the BBC. (The slide show can, however, still be viewed on Youtube if you missed it).

Pompous aspirations aside, though, the disc, I do believe, is a good one and probably my favourite so far. The idea behind the title *We Play For Food* came from our need to make our Glastonbury stints pay: our tramping around the site, double bass on back and amps in a wheelbarrow, calling at every bar and cafe that had a stage and a PA and swapping our services for food and/or drinks was the inspiration.

The tour that followed the launch, throughout the spring and summer of '17, was every bit as knackering for these two middle-aged blokes as had been the last one. The difference this time, though, was that we were slowly beginning to get noticed. Opportunities were opening up that hadn't been there before as we were bounced up to bigger stages and trusted to play near bigger names. In the May we opened for Adam Ant (the man who'd first inspired me to both write and perform) at the Watford Colosseum. In the August we shared a billing with another 80s legend: Toyah, at The Winter Gardens in Blackpool, at another festival that had previously ignored us. The map board in Donna's office began gaining pins in lots of new places as we pushed ever further forward...

...to where, though?

2018 marks the tenth anniversary of The Antipoet. We've done a lot in that time; far more than we'd ever expected to do; far more than either of us has ever done in all the bands we've played with. We've had a lot of fun and I hope we've still more to come.

We didn't start out with a goal so no one can say that we haven't achieved it, but where are we going? Who knows; who cares!

We're just artists...

'We want Antipoet next year, otherwise I'm sure there'll be a riot from the audience.'
—Anna Harriott, Arts Programmer Larmer Tree Festival, July 2016

45

Glastonbury Programme shot 2014 (Jonathan Lambton)

Ledbury Festival 2011 (Jo Bell)

46

Green Gathering Chesptow 2016 (Catherine Lliffe)

Larmer Tree Festival 2015 (Sebastian Schofield)

5. The Glorious Three Year Plan

(Or The Seven Year Itch, If You Prefer)

"Eyeliner, triangle and a double bass have never been funnier!"
—Word of Mouth, September 2010

As I've already said, he and I have both played in numerous bands over the years, racking up, The Bard only knows, how many gigs between us, both at home and abroad. There have obviously been some standouts amongst these, but never so many as we've collected as equal parts of The Antipoet. I'd put a lot of that down to the fact that with bands, one venue is often quite similar to the next; one pub's back room blurring seamlessly into the next, quite out of necessity, as bands require a certain amount of space along with power points for amps and instruments, lighting, a PA and, lest we forget, more than a little room for their burgeoning egos.

The Antipoet, on the other hand, is a much more compact and far less demanding beast to take out, despite that bloody double bass! We can and we have played the most eclectic and often ridiculous 'venues'; sometimes just to be able to say that we have done; it being a particular penchant of Donna's to accept the most unlikely of gigs in order to 'colour' our CV. Like the retired and decidedly unseaworthy minesweeper that we played on the Thames, down Deptford way, that had been nailed to the quayside in order to stop it from sinking; to the drawing room of a rather plush town house in Ladbroke Grove, for a ninetieth birthday soiree (where we had to go down two flights of stairs and use the tradesman's entrance, then go through the scullery and up another two flights, in order to come out on the inside of the door that we had first knocked on because; as mere poets, we couldn't be seen to walk through the same door as the gentry!) We've played art galleries;

48

churches; a couple of broad-minded schools; the minstrel's gallery of Liverpool Town Hall; Silverstone race track for the 2010 Grand Prix, (where we were support to a kilted pipe band); the window of an exclusive boutique in Teddington High Street; a canal boat on The Grand Union as it passed through Uxbridge; libraries galore; book shops; a record shop; a shop selling extremely expensive glass sculptures (very scary!); an alleyway; various high streets; hotels; tents of every hue, shape and size; a stately home; pubs, oh so many pubs; night clubs; an old cinema; a golf club; a bowls club; teashops by the ton; theatres; the international space station (or did I dream that one?); the back of a lorry; a furniture showroom; an off-licence; a swimming pool; a cow shed; a dungeon; several farms; a sports hall; a tree house; an Indian restaurant; a vegan restaurant; a clearing in a wood; and the list goes on, as very rarely (as you might have noticed) do we turn anything down! It's been one of the best bits of doing what we do, over the years, that we are not restricted by where we do it. We'd still like to do a castle, a submarine and the end of a pier, if anyone out there has any contacts...

It was the back end of 2015, having enjoyed a successful summer season, including our fourth sojourn to The Edinburgh Fringe, that we finally realised that we might've been onto something. We hadn't really noticed it before. Yes, we'd had our fair share of luck in recent years, but we've been tarts of the boards for a long time; we've both done other things over the decades that looked like they might have been about to make us, but you soon learn not to take things too seriously. Who knows when it might all come tumbling down?

But when people whom you've never met before come up to you at a gig that you've never played before, in a town you've never even been to before and ask you if you've got a new album out yet, suddenly one's senses become alerted. You tingle when you hear people reciting your words back to you during a gig and when they all call for a different favourite when offered an encore, one bristles with pride; though I do wish people wouldn't do that pointy thing.

You really start to notice when the heckles start getting personal:

'Tell us about Attila, go on!'

As you'll no doubt be aware, if you've been reading this book in a linear fashion, we've been making this shit up as we've gone along: it would be churlish of us to pretend otherwise and we can't be the first speciality act to have just 'gone with the flow'? But maybe, we thought, maybe it was about time we started working to a plan...

And thus The Glorious Three Year Plan was born!

We're both getting on in life, that's hardly a secret: 'The wrong side of fifty', so the poem goes, 'so we can't 'ang about'. So isn't it about time that we made up our minds and did something about it? Alright, we're in it for the fun, that's ultimately why we do it, very few get to do poetry for any other reason, but what if there was a chance of us actually, 'Making it': becoming a name in our field? Could we afford to let that chance, however slim and fleeting, pass us by without making a token grab for it? At our time of life we may not get another shot. Fame and fortune should and could never be an artiste's sole raison d'etre , but come on, let's be honest, it's never that far from your mind, is it?

I can look back on so many past chapters of my life and say: "If only I'd given that project a little more time" or "I wish I'd been more committed to that particular idea". Of course, I'll never know if I would have made it as a pop star if only I'd tried a bit harder and made the compromises that those A & R men had suggested; or a playwright; or a director; or

a...

The Antipoet, this beaty poetry malarkey that we trek around the country some 150-odd times a year, has become an integral part of all three of our lives. It often feels like we've been peddling it forever, but we really haven't. It feels natural to both Ian and me: a perfect fit for our characters and our questionable talents, so we're going to give this one everything we've got; we owe it to our younger selves!

In 2010, whilst punting ourselves and the RRRANTS crew at The Brighton Fringe, I went so far as to have our logo (as designed by my

50

good friend, Paul Solomons) tattooed on my shoulder. My thoughts were that, regardless of whether or not we were ever going to hit the big time, I wanted to make sure that I never forgot how much being a part of this act had meant to me. Yes, I'd had a few at the time, but I've never regretted it.

"You do realise," my father warned me, shaking his head at my middle-aged naivety, "that you've got that for life, now?"

I smiled wryly. I do that when I'm being patronised.

"Not really," I told him, inadvertently reminding him of his own mortality in the process, "more than half of it's already over."

He shut up after that. You'll noticed from our *Bards* tour photos and our *Play for Food* publicity shots, that Ian has also since made the ultimate artistic commitment. We suggested that Donna might like to join our exclusive club, but she told us to Fuck Off and grow up; mouth like a sewer, that one.

When I started writing this book, we were exactly three years from having been at this for a decade. We've achieved quite a bit in those seven years, more than either of us had ever expected, but should we have done more in the time that we've had, we asked ourselves? Were we slacking? Was there not more that we could be doing whilst we still had our wits, most of our hair and our own teeth?

After careful deliberation, we decided that there was. So we laid it out: the three of us, sat there in Ian's ex-wife's campervan; the one that we'd been using until her goodwill toward the father of her children finally dried up. We'd do three tours, we decided, six months a piece on a one-per-year basis up to our tenth anniversary. Let's do all the places that we'd gone down well in the past, we said, plus let's dig out all the leads we'd been offered along the way, but hadn't yet followed due to our prior commitments to our monthly RRRANTS nights, which would now have to go on hold for a while in order to facilitate the added workload.

So, with a stand-in drafted to cover some of my monthly adult story nights in Richmond, (thank you, Simon) and a thump of dep bass players (I'm sure that's the collective noun for them; it's either that or a "whinge" or is it a "spank"? I know it's a "wank of poets") to cover Ian for his various bands, we set sail for Cambridge to record *The Bards of Bugger All*: step one of our "Everything we can do" plan. A year of touting that around and we'd be back up to Mark's to record another ten tracks for *We Play For Food*, which we would follow in March 2017 with a second tour, then in '18 we'd publish this book and do a third tour to tout that. If The Antipoet weren't your "go to" beat poets by then, then we probably never would be.

We'd toured before, of course, as those of you who supported us on our 2013 "Rhythm Method" tour, and Mark Niel (Poet Laureate of Milton Keynes; no, that's not a joke) will attest. We'd been attempting to lift our names above those of our peers then too—those who also did a lot of gigs, but relatively randomly—by branding our own run of randomly spaced gigs "a tour". (It's all in the marketing, y'see.) It had taught us quite a bit. Our intention that time had just been to lift our profile: to head out proactively, playing areas that we'd never played and where the punters didn't know us, and to that end it had worked. Uncertain as to whether or not we had the clout to do it on our tods, we chose a running mate for company and contrast, someone as far distanced from our own stylings as possible. (I don't know why, it just seemed a sound move at the time!) Enter Mark Niel: Bard in 1970's bank manager form, but the most professional and consistently reliable poet that we knew.

It was an eye-opener for all of us: twenty-one dates, scattered around the country, ending with a solid week's run at that year's Edinburgh Fringe in an attempt to call it "International" (a dodgy assertion that we also made for *Bards* and *Food* with our weekends in Wales!)

Now, Mark's a decent chap, even if we don't share a school of thought or a sense of style. We'd known him from the poeting circuit. He's a dedicated and conscientious performer whom I've never seen give anything less than his best. He'd helped us out a few years earlier when he had been forced to drop out of a show at the Buxton Fringe and had kindly nominated us to fill his laced up brown brogues. Without that gig, we would never have been chosen for the next Ledbury festival, from which we gained so much useful publicity; mainly from one particularly well-established poet (whom I shan't name), who was so horrified that we'd been booked there at all, that she moaned to the press and anybody else who'd listen about "lowering standards at a professional poetry event"; in the process, unwittingly imbuing us with an unprecedented degree of hyperbole and ensuring that our show sold out, giving us one of our most rewarding nights ever. No such thing as bad publicity!

We split the Rhythm Method shows into two halves, each taking it in turns to headline, but always kicking off and finishing with a specially written three-hander. The most frustrating part of this tour was this split. It meant that neither us nor Mark ever got time to really get into our sets. It might have worked for some people, I've seen a lot of Ed Fringe shows do this, but it didn't so much for us; hence the reason we now tour on our own, or, when a little gentle fluffing is required, enlist the genius of Mr Poeterry to work his chaotic charm for us.

But back to the plan. Two albums in two years was a bit tight, many said, Ian being one of them, I remember, but imagine doing the same set at every gig for months on end: edgy poetry very quickly starts to lose its edge. By the end of the Rhythm Method tour, we probably knew Mr Niel's set as well as we did our own; ditto, of course, for him with ours, and we'd certainly seen him with his clothes off once too often! (Actually once is too often).

And audiences get bored too. They might like what you do, but there's only so many times you can hear the same set until you start wishing the act would cock it up, just to break the monotony. For me it's all about the new: writing more and seeing people's responses to what you've written, as it's yours truly who's task it is to come up with the words. You'll know by having read this far into this book, that I can go on and on and on and on.......

Talking of the book—the one that you currently have in your

53

hand—this was to be the final part of that big plan: phase three of let's see what we can achieve in ten years. People often come up after a gig and say, " Which of your CDs has all the good ones on?" By which we presume them to mean, our most popular pieces. They've only got the one fiver on them, they weren't expecting to spend any money tonight and so "can they just have the one that's got the set they've just heard on it, please?" Our original thought was to do just that, but then we thought "where would that leave our back catalogue sales?" So we decided to publish a book instead, with the words to our most popular pieces printed out so that you can see what I'm supposed to be ranting when I get it wrong. I thought I'd add a few words by way of an introduction, but as you can see, I got a bit carried away. We have put a "best of" disc together for you, but it's a DVD instead of a CD, so you won't be able to play it in your car, or download the bugger, and you will still have to buy all the discs if you want to play 'Rant-along-an-Antipoet'. (We're not stupid.)

By the time you read this we will have begun recording our seventh collection, currently under the working title of, *Punk Uncle*: another ten beat-driven diatribes on the state of the world as told by two past-their-primers. We hope you enjoyed reading our story. Where we go and what we do from here is largely up to you. Join our Arsebook page or follow us on Twatter and stay in touch, or come and see us at a gig somewhere and tell us what you think. We really don't bite.

"The Antipoet look like an old style punk, aided by a double bass player, booted in six-inch heels. (Their) hilarious anarchic beat ranting on virtually any subject delighted an audience rammed to the gunwales."

— (Larmer Tree Festival) Bournemouth Echo July 2016

Poetry and Words flyer 2017 (Samantha Sweetland)

Publicity shot with manager Donna 2017 (Jonathan Lambton)

Rec Rock Festival 2016 (Donna Ray)

56

6. Punk And The Art Of Post Modernist Poetry

(An article by Paul Eccentric, reprinted from the November 2016 issue of the 'Tuesday Club' e-magazine, with permission)

"Really, really ace! I like what you do"
—Ray Peacock, comedian, FUBAR Radio, February 2015

Two weeks ago (as I write this), The Antipoet, of whom I am the mouthy half, concluded a fifty-date promo tour for our latest album: *BARDS OF BUGGER ALL* with a gig in a manor house with llamas in the front garden, on the outskirts of Yeovil, Somerset. Just before we hit the boards that night, as the turn booked to accompany a feast's main course, the promoter for said event sidled up to me and asked: 'Alright if I introduce you boys as "punk poets"?'

It was the first time that we'd been billed as such all year. We'd played two weddings, a care home for the terminally bewildered, a hostel for the homeless and even a proper punk festival without anyone feeling the need to pre-empt us with a genre specific disclaimer. Now don't get me wrong here, I don't have a problem with that tag per se and I told him so. It's been said before and, as intro's go, it's as good a label as any for whatever it is that we do do, but personally, I've never really thought of us in such succinct and particular terms. I did, however, for the remainder of that weekend…

So what is a Punk Poet, exactly?

Atilla The Stockbroker is my idea of a punk poet. He's got all the proper credentials that I would associate with such an angry moniker: he's ranty; he's shouty; he's political; he was even there at the start of it all, but who knows: he may even take umbrage at my describing him in that way.

It's all a matter of opinion, isn't it?

It's been said that we look more 'Goth' than punk and we do tend to use a sod of a lot more words per piece than your average three-chord punk anthem employs and, on the wrong side of fifty, some may even consider us too old to be 'punk'. Okay, we do tend to rant'n rail a bit and we do like to fuck with received poetic convention, but does that make us 'punk' or just middle class; middle-aged whingers?

Back in the day, 'back when I were a lad', things were so much simpler. Things either 'were' a thing or they 'weren't'. We took what we were given and we made the best of it.

We listened to the 'Breakfast Show' on Radio 1, every morning before school, with the likes of Noel Edmonds, Dave Lee Travis and Mike Read feeding us the 'hits' of the moment: those records that the BBC (by 'special' arrangement with the larger, more influential record companies of the day) deemed suitable for primetime broadcast, whilst we chowed down on our Shreddies and warm milk. Well, we didn't know any better, did we! Remember: these were the days before the advent of the internet; before YouTube; before multi channel TV; before commercial radio had been allowed to prosper and before Channel 4 arrived with 'The Tube'. How would we have known that there was something else out there, bubbling just below the surface: something that didn't fit comfortably with the prevalent middle class pop stylings of those privileged enough to have had private music tutelage; something a tad rougher around the gills than we'd previously been used to: rawer and less forgiving, undeserving of our attention; something crude, rude and as arrogant as that which it chose to usurp?

But as this prepubescent was about to discover: there's often more to this world than they'd have you believe…

I was nine when it all kicked off: too young to understand, apparently, too young to 'get it' and certainly too young to join in. Not too young, though, to notice that something was afoot and not so naïve that I wasn't able to recognise that something that I'd already both seen and identified with elsewhere.

I wasn't very popular at school. It didn't help that I wasn't very good at anything. Nothing came easily to me. I know now that this was due to my dyslexia, but at the time I'd simply accepted the explanation offered me: that I was simply 'thick' and lazy. Dyslexia meant that I saw things differently to those around me. I questioned everything everybody told me because I couldn't understand why there was only a right or a wrong way of doing everything. What if there was a different way, I'd wondered; a way that works just as well, but that nobody's thought of yet? There wasn't, I was reliably informed by the powers that be. I claimed not to like any of the things that I was expected to like: football, fighting and the music that we were being force fed, but I was just being awkward, apparently. However, things were about to change for me; I was about to discover something that would make sense of the way I felt: a mood, an ethos, a fundament that would inform everything that I was from that moment forward. Ladies and gentlemen, I give you...punk rock!

My best friend at the time was The Doctor (Doctor Who, to the uninitiated amongst you). Of course, he didn't know that. How could he have done? He was a fictional character.

Tom Baker had been The Doctor when sentience had first struck me and total absorption in the mythos of the programme was what got me through the horrors of day-to-day school life. Here was a bloke who didn't give a shit about how things were supposed to be done: an anarchist by the term's very definition! Fashion had no effect on him whatsoever, neither did class appreciation nor the petty rules that kept the little man down and the bully calling the shots. All he cared about was fairness and equality and he'd stand beside anyone who wanted to fight for those principle tenets. I wanted to be like him. Actually, I wanted to be him, but I could accept the former. I looked at the world and I couldn't see a place in it for me, so I lost myself to the wandering Time Lord's adventures on telly and in print. Reality had very little hold on me back then.

That was until the first of December 1976. I can't remember why I'd been watching a boring, current affairs programme; it hadn't been my thing at all. It'd probably been my dad's idea: his way of trying to get me to engage with the world; to bring me down from the clouds and get me interested in real life issues, but for the purposes of this narrative, I'm not going to blame the old man: I'm going to put it down to serendipity.

Anyway, there I was sat in front of the box with my jam sandwich and my orange squash when Bill Grundy, former footballer, now turned TV interviewer, had invited 'The Sex Pistols' onto his 'Today' programme.

I'd heard that name bandied around at school: 'Sex Pistols'. It sounded rude. It sounded like something that I wasn't supposed to know about. I liked them already! They were a 'pop group'; though not like anything we'd ever heard before. Their records had been banned from the radio, so I'd been yet to hear what all the fuss had been about.

It's an infamous story, so I won't patronise you by recalling the details of the event that ruined Grundy's career, and introduced the wider world to punk rock, but suffice it to say; the way I recall it, anyway: Grundy encouraged guitarist Steve Jones and singer Johnny Rotten to use the 'F' word on national television. He goaded them. He'd bullied them, to my eyes and they'd delivered, and that's how punk rock came into my (and many other people's) lives.

'THE FILTH & THE FURY!' ran The Guardian the next morning, every other daily taking a similar, establishment-defending stance. My dad was as outraged as the rest of the country and in that instant, punk rock became something evil and depraved: a byword for all that was wrong with the world. There are those who, forty years on, will still argue that 'The Grundy Incident' killed the fledgling underground movement by bringing it out in the open like that, but for most of us that interview was our baptism into a world of infinite possibility! There WAS a third way after all!

I mentioned before that the BBC had 'banned' some of The Sex Pistols' records. This presumptuous practice was something unique to its time. The banning of anything makes that thing even more desirable for those for whom that something has been denied. It creates controversy and fuels interest like nothing else. The banning of a record only served to publicise such a product far beyond its rights and its means. Besides, 'banned' in these instances is a total misnomer. They refused to play them on the BBC, but you could still buy them in the shops! It was brilliant marketing! People rushed out to buy them in their droves without even knowing whether what they so craved was actually any good or not.

Suddenly punk was everywhere. If you'd been reading the papers at that time you could have been excused for thinking that the world had been coming to a bloody and premature end, but from where I was standing it was the exact opposite! The BBC ban may well have boosted record sales by a mile and brought this new anti-style to the attention of the masses, but our own household ban of punk rock records, whilst having a much smaller impact on the world at large, would leave an unbelievable mark on the life of one individual: namely me. I very much doubt that I would ever have put pen to paper if I hadn't, over the years that followed, bought records by the likes of Ian Dury & The Blockheads (banned by my parents for use of the word 'bastard'); The Boomtown Rats (also banned by my parents for supposedly glorifying murder); The Sex Pistols (again, banned by my parents, this time for most of the lyrics in 'Friggin' In The Rigging'); The Damned; The Ruts; Sham 69; The Gymslips; The Leighton Buzzards; Tenpole Tudor; Siouxie & The Banshees (hated by my father); The Toy Dolls; Serious Drinking; and never ever forgetting: Adam & The Antz!

Punk Rock had shown me that there was another way to be; that it was alright to be different: in fact, being different was to be celebrated!

It'd shown me that I'd been right to recognise The Doctor as the ultimate anti-establishment antihero and that yes: I could be like him! It'd shown me that a dyslexic, untitled, secondary-modern-educated dreamer with a total lack of academic qualifications could achieve everything he set out to achieve without compromise.

It'd shown me that a punk attitude was something to crow about.

Like I say, I mulled that question over the weekend and came to the conclusion that yes, we are a punk poetry act.

PS: *I had a word with Attila The Stockbroker after writing this piece and I asked him for his views on the subject of Punk Poetry. This is what he said to me…*

'For me it's simple: I summed it up years ago, back in the '80s when I was first starting out. Punk is an attitude: it's not about the noise you make or what you look like, it's about doing things on your own terms; making your own way and not being told what to do by the mainstream, but of course being part of your own scene as well; working as a catalyst within it and doing everything you can do to help other performers within it (as long as they're good on stage and have good values). I am happy to be described as a "punk poet" because I came out of the punk scene and although my material is very different now, the old DIY ethos is at the centre of everything I do. Punk poetry is existentialism in words after a few pints. And of course, on the very few occasions when I do behave like an arsehole, (you were actually the recipients of the last one I can remember) I have an excuse, 'cause I'm quite volatile and so is punk.'

—Atilla The Stockbroker, October 2016, speaking to Paul Eccentric.

"Sweet as strawberries; sharp as lemon barley water."
—Jo Bell, Ledbury Festival, July 2011

Shooting the Animal Antiks video 2016 (Donna Ray)

Strawberry Fair with the ex-bard of Northampton Justin Thyme 2017 (Donna Ray)

The Antipoet *cartoon 2015 (Samantha Sweetland)*

The Antipoet Christmas Message *2014 (Samantha Sweetland)*

7. Housekeeping

Ian and I take a 50/50 writing credit on all of the Antipoet pieces, regardless of which of us came up with the riff; the title or the inspiration for a particular track (except for 'Two Gentlemen Duellers'; which was written by Paul before we became a partnership, and the skits on 'We Play For Food', which were also written by Paul).

The majority of the words are Paul's, with Ian's 'editing suggestions' being acknowledged approximately twice per album, and the finalised bass lines being Ian's, as he's the one who knows how to play the bloody thing, after all!

The words in this book were written by Paul between March 2015 and September 2017 and edited by Donna, after an alcohol fuelled anecdote storming session involving all three of us. Any resemblance to persons living or dead is probable, but unproveable. Anyone who feels that any of our poems are about them is just vain.

With Kung Fu Panda 2017 (Donna Ray)

Worcestershire LitFest and Fringe 2016 (Donna Ray)

Bards of
BUGGER ALL
Tour 2016

23rd Feb Black's Club SOHO
16th March Cook Hotel STONY STRATFORD
18th March NN Contemporary Art NORTHAMPTON
1st April The Junction CAMBRIDGE
5th April The Book Club HACKNEY
6th April The Small Horse Inn BRISTOL
7th April Komedia BRIGHTON
12th April The Old Fire Station OXFORD
13th April Horse & Stables WATERLOO
24th April Coco Cafe CROXLEY GREEN
30th April Trestle Theatre ST ALBANS
14th May Devonshire Arms CAMBRIDGE

21st May RICKMANSWORTH FESTIVAL
4th June STRAWBERRY FAIR CAMBRIDGE
5th June GLASTONWICK FESTIVAL
15th June Raising The Awen NORTHAMPTON
18th June WORCESTERSHIRE LITFEST
24th-26th June GLASTONBURY FESTIVAL
4th July The Horns WATFORD
15th-17th July LARMERTREE FESTIVAL
29th July CAMP BESTIVAL
4th-6th Aug THE GREEN GATHERING
26th-29th Aug BLYTH POWER ASHES
22nd Sept Mill Brewery TOWCESTER
25th Sept REC ROCK FESTIVAL

Tour Poster 2017 (Elliot O'Brart)

8. Rant-Along-An-Antipoet

This selection has been taken from the following albums, all released on, 'RRRANTS Records'.

Tights not Stockings	2011	RRRCD01
Hanging With Poets	2012	RRRCD06
Random Words in a Random Order	2013	RRRCD12
Ere's One for The Kiddies	2014	RRRCD22
The Bards of Bugger All!	2016	RRRCD28
We Play For Food	2017	RRRCD30

Available from: http://rrrants.org/the-antipoet
Or available to download on: http://www.theantipoet.co.uk/

We're Artists

We're artists!
we're of a sensitive disposition,
we can't really be expected
to work in our condition,
because we're special
and we've got a lot to give;
we shouldn't really have to
prostitute ourselves so we can live.

Do you have *any* idea
of the depths of pain and torment
that your average artiste endures
for your entertainment?
And we're not your average, oh no;
we put our souls into our work,
imbuing our creations
with a quality of quirk.
And are we respected;
(Not really, no.)
rewarded for our artistry,
celebrated for our dedicated mastery
and given the freedom
from the drudge of the daily grind
to express our poignant stirrings,
for the good of all mankind?

I tell you we're artists!
We're of a sensitive disposition,
we can't really be expected
to work in our condition;
what we have is special

and we're doing it for you!
We are who we are
and what we say is what we do!

So punters take pity
on the struggling artiste:
put some pennies in our hat
or buy our books and discs at least
and save us from day jobs,
from sullying our hands;
repetitive strain,
numbing the brain
aren't things that a poet understands.
And where's our Arts Council grant
for doing what we do so well?
Our government encouragement
t'help us to excel?
Don't make us work to earn our crust;
we need our time to ponder on
the trials of our existence
and put it in poetry and song.

We're artists!
We're of a sensitive disposition;
we can't really be expected
to work in our condition
because we're special:
we've got a lot to give,
we shouldn't really have to
prostitute ourselves so we can live.
We shouldn't really have to prostitute Ian so we can live, but we do!

Two Gentlemen Duellers

Two gentlemen of breeding
found themselves in some dispute,
when a trifling breach of etiquette
impugned the one's repute.

For honour to be satisfied a duel was to be fought;
the challenged chose the method
and a blindfold, just for sport.

The other threw his gauntlet down and challenged with a curse:
'to the DEATH, but through the medium
of the rhyming verse':

'Sir, you are a rotter; a bounder and a cad!'
Ssir, your dog; your mother and your valet
I have had!'
'Sir, you are a blaggard; a dandy and a ponce!'
'Sir, you are anorchous and your father is a nonce!'
'Sir, you are an oik! You are a varlet and a cuss!'
'Sir, is that your wife or just some poxed rhinoceros?'
'Sir, you are a jackanapes, if I must be so blunt?'
'Sir, you have the aspect of a ladies bottom front!'
'Sir, that last remark not only rankles, it's a lie!'
'Sir, I dub thee loser! Take your leave: fuck off and die!'

Sign Of The Times/Gimp Night

It's the 21st century we're living in;
whether we like it or not,
'though it isn't the future that we'd hoped to see;
it's the one that we bloody well got.
It should all be robots and jetpacks and clones and silver jumpsuits by
now;
driverless cars
and time-shares on Mars:
Tomorrow's World said we'd know how.

We were expecting our future to be
from sci-fi and fantasy hewn:
all rolling pavements
and pills for our food;
a retirement plot on the moon.
Instead we've been cheated;
bankrupted and fleeced
and we're on this austerity drive,
forced to diversify just to get by,
we've all had to adapt to survive…

So we're playing…
Gimp Night down at The Fighting Cocks:
they've got whips'n chains'n bondage and a fondle box;
the swingers have the basement;
there are poets in the snug,
all in the hope they'll buy some beer in a straight glass or a jug!
So, we'll do Gimp Night down at The Fighting Cocks;
it's Tranny Night on Sundays for the men in frocks.
Every first Tuesday
they have midget fights:

it shifts more crisps than karaoke or pop quiz nights!

When I was young a review said of me:
"this boy, he's going to go far;
he straddles the line between madness and genius;
he is a natural born star".
The world was my oyster;
I would've been rich,
if what he'd predicted'd come through.
I'd've been touring the globe;
I'd've been someone not nobody,
standing here talking to you.

But nothing's turned out quite how we thought it might;
our best laid plans all came t'now't,
so we'll do what we must do
like everyone else
because we've all got bills to pay out.
That's why we're not precious 'bout the gigs that we do,
we've played strip clubs; shop windows;
cafés;
we've busked in the street,
just so that we could eat:
he'll do anything as long as it pays…

So we'll play
Gimp Night down at The Fighting Cocks,
where the landlord's into the spirit taking cattle-prod shocks;
there are jelly wrestling virgins out on the patio;
there's a black mass in the function room so the lights are down low.
They want us for:
Gimp Night down at The Fighting Cocks;
they've got every fetish catered for

with a free glass of Hock.
On Thursdays it's the sewing circle,
but not every third;
that's when the real perverts show up for a night of spoken word!

They're doing a
Gimp Night down at your local pub;
they serve pints'n shots'n measures
an' lubricants by the tub.
It might not be traditional
like darts, but they've got t'thrive
and it's keeping them in business
and turns like us alive!
Oh yes it's
Gimp Night down at The Fighting Cocks
so grab yourself a mask
and a pint and some PVC jocks.
It's Gimp Night down at The Fighting Cocks:
it's a sign of the times,
the last orders bell chimes…
    Well…
It's better than ten-a-penny covers bands churning out second hand
rock!

'Ere's One For The Kiddies

Little baby, so innocent, so new.
Little baby, with it all yet to go through.
Little baby, there's so much I must tell you,
'cause Mum and Dad are lying to you,
That's what parents do.
Have they told you you're beautiful,
coochi, coochi, coo?
Though you clearly look like
Winston Churchill straining for a poo.
Did they tell you they'd be there for you
throughout your early years
and did they dump you in a nursery
and get on with their careers?
Have they told you that you are their special little gift?
Well you're not, you were an accident,
one night when they were spliffed!

Ere's one for the kiddies,
don't believe them when they say
we'll love you whatever, even if you turn out gay.
Little baby, so delicate and pure.
Little baby, so naïve and so unsure.
Little baby, listen up so you'll be sure
you'll know bullshit when you smell it
'cause you've so much to endure.

Did they tell you that Daddy had been a naughty boy,
which was why Mummy had to whip him and insert that saveloy?
Did they tell you that Mummy had hurt her bum?
Which is why Daddy kissed it better
and had to rub it with his thumb.

75

What did they tell you about that
Darth Vader mask you saw
and what apparently wasn't
a light sabre in Mummy's special drawer?

Ere's one for the kiddies don't believe what they tell you:
the more believable it sounds;
the less likely it's true.

Little baby, so trusting and so cute.
Little baby, far too young to be astute.
Little baby, you will grow up to refute
everything they've told you
and you might just prosecute.
They will tell you not to take sweets
from men that you don't know
unless they're wearing a false beard and whisper, 'ho, ho, ho';
that you won't go to heaven
if you don't eat up your greens
and that they'll treat you as an adult
when you get to eighteen;
to believe in Father Christmas
the tooth fairy, Jesus Krist,
but what these figures have in common is that none of them exist!

Ere's one for the kiddies:
the biggest lies they tell are...
You'll die if you put your finger in that socket, son;
dogshit doesn't taste like chocolate
and never step out into the road without looking both ways.

We Play For Food

There's not a lot of money in performance poetry:
the medium relies upon our generosity.
They think we're happy just to be here;
punt our services for free,
because we can't write if we're not living in abject poverty.
They say they don't wish to offend us
by paying us a fee,
as they understand we're martyrs to our 'integrity'.
That's why we poets are the paupers of the art world hegemony,
but on the plus side we don't earn enough to pay VAT.
We play for food...
We take payment
in sandwiches and chips.
We play for food...
You give us buns, we'll give you beaty verse'n quips.
We play for food...
Don't try to palm us off with crisps and humous dips,
'cause that's just rude!
that's not food, that's just fuckin' rude!

And whilst we're not averse to turning out for the odd charity;
there's a limit to our selflessness and
our philanthropy.
We still have outgoings; expenses;
a vestige of dignity, we need to clothe ourselves in velvet; lace and shiny
PVC.
It would be diff'rent if we were a band
or doing stand-up comedy:
profess'nal entertainers to be taken seriously.
They should give subsidies to poets for our incapacity;
recognise our inclination as a disability.

We'll play for drinks…
Stand our bar bill and we'll rant away all night.
We'll play for drinks…
Though y'might regret that:
we've got quite the appetite.
We'll play for drinks…
The more we sup:
the more polite and erudite you'll find my links.

We'll play for sex…
Well… it's always worth a try.
we'll play for sex…
If you've run out
of sandwiches and pie.
We'll play for sex…
These are your options if you find yourself cash shy,
we still take cheques.
We play for food…
He'll eat anything you put in front of him.
We play for food…
But I don't do cheese and I'm a vegetarian.
We play for food!
Check our rider for preferred ingredients,
it can be viewed at: theantipoet/weplayforfood!

1420Mhz

He wrote a single word in the margin.

One word: three letters and an exclamation mark.

'Wow!'

And it seemed so inadequate for the sentiment that he wanted to express.

'Wow!'

A word coined to convey the feeling of profound exclamation.

For that was how he felt as his mind struggled to digest the information in front of him,

just 'Wow!'

'Is there anybody out there?' he had asked, as people had been asking since time immemorial, 'can anybody hear me;

is there anyone listening in the wider galaxy?

'Are we alone; are we unique, as the world's religions preach or merely pebbles on sentience beach?'

To know the answers to these questions would be, 'Wow!'

That would change *everything*!

To know that ours was not the only form of life in existence might just have humbled us into accepting our own *less* than significance;

drawn a veil over our reliance on religion an superstition;

heralded the dawn of a new era in human evolution.

He had sent a message: a coded riddle.

He had sent it out into the unknown.

He had reasoned that any alien life with the intelligence to receive such a signal would also be capable of translating his message

and of responding in like.

'Wow!'

To be able to commune with a species from another world. To drag humanity kicking and screaming from the parochial isms of a stagnating society and to be able to nudge it toward a future devoid of such arrogant piety.

'Wow!'

1420Mhz was his message: the frequency at which hydrogen, the most common element in the universe, emits radiation.

A simple message. A pulse that merely asks: 'do we understand one another;

are we on the same wavelength?'

A simple 'wow' scribbled in the margin, a 'wow' as he sees the results of the test:

At 1420Mhz-a discernible narrowband pulse.

Received and understood.

'Yes we do'.

So, wow, yes, wow!

What else could he have written?

What better word was there?

His peers had agreed that there would be little room for debate and that a signal received at 1420Mhz would be accepted as an attempt by persons, extra-terrestrial, to communicate, as no natural phenomena could incidentally replicate the traits

of a wow result.

And yet…

This is a true story and the' Wow! Signal' was received in 1977.

So where are our neighbours;

where is our brave new future

and did our hero ever receive a second signal at 1420 MHz?

We'll probably never know.

The telescope was dismantled shortly afterwards and the observatory flattened to make way for a golf course.

Wow!

Festivals, I Shit'em

It's wellies; tents and chemical khazee season.
We're playing in a tent in a field
for no good reason.
There was a band on first whom I thought I knew from Top Of The
Pops in 1972;
a poet who has obviously never been kissed, excuse me whilst I nip out
and slash my wrist.
'Oh, would you come, boys, and play at our fest?
As beaty poets go we think you're the best.
We 'aven't sold many tickets,
so we'll 'ave t'owe ya'
but you'll sell CDs and it's good exposure.

It's wellies; tents and chemical khazee season.
We're playing in a tent in a field
and it's fuckin' freezing.
Where the term 'fast food' refers to the speed that it travels through our
system and we start to need
the khazees, we smelt as we arrived
and are bound to be bog roll and water deprived.
'We were gunna' hold it on our mate's dad's farm; we really couldn't see
how we'd'a done any harm,
but his dad said, 'No, now get off moi land!'
so it's my mum's garden and some
smaller bands.'

It's wellies; tents and chemical khazee season.
That's not a veggie burger, it's a bun with some lettuce leaves on.
Home brewed cider that looks like it was peed; a ten year old selling
home grown weed;
crusties in tutus and tossers on stilts;

The Antipoet in bondage kilts!
It's wellies; tents and chemical khazee season.
There's only one act I want to see
and we're on when he's on.

It's wellies; tents and chemical khazee season.
We're playing in a tent in a field and it's fuckin' freezin'.
It's wellies; tents and chemical khazee season.
There's never anyone in this fuckin' field when we's on.
It's wellies; tents and chemical khazee season.

The Wrong Question

I heard it at the counter
just a moment ago:
some hipster bearded 'geezer' who
ought to know better:
'can I get a skinny latte t'go?'
He caught it from an American television show.
He thinks it makes him sound 'cool'
and in the groove;
he doesn't understand why we might
disapprove.
Go-getter wouldn't let a
bit of antediluvian grammar
spoil his patter whilst he's making his move.

Can I get a coffee;
can I, can I get a coffee;
can I, can I get a coffee?
Can you?
I don't know!

'Please may I have one?'
is what we say;
a little bit of courtesy goes a long way,
'cause this is England, where politeness pays
and we don't say 't'go' we say: 'to take a fuckin' way'!
He wears his baggy trousers at half mast,
from whence we get the slang term:
half-arsed,
trendsetter to the letter: an iconoclast,
he doesn't have the time for a proper breakfast.
He's on the go; he's in'n out;

he's got somewhere t'be;
he's looking at his phone
whilst he is talking t'me.
He ate an olive, feta, pumpkin seeded
Panini and mumbled 'cheers'
instead of thank you: intolerably!
Can I get a coffee;
can I, can I get a coffee;
can I, can I get a coffee?
Can you;
How should I know?

That's not the question you meant to ask;
you're showing us the ignorance in which you bask.
If it was me, I wouldn't serve you;
I'd make you say it properly,
it's not 't'go' it's: 't' take away'!
Can I get a coffee;
can I, can I get a coffee;
can I, can I get a coffee?
Can he, I don't know!
He's asking: can he get a coffee;
can he, can he get a coffee;
can he, can he get a coffee?
Can he?

Random Words In A Random Order

There's a woman on the stage;
she likes to think that she's a poet,
she's got something on her mind
and she's attempting to bestow it,
but she's not a friend of brevity
and editing's beyond her,
so it spews like wordy vomit
and my mind begins to ponder..
What the fuck,
What the fuck,
What the fuck is she on about?
What the fuck,
What the fuck,
What the fuck is she on about?
What the fuck,
What the fuck,
What the fuck is she on about?

It's just random words in a random order;
random words in a random order.
Random words in a random order:
don't clap because she'll think that you are trying to reward her!

There's a bloke up on the stage;
he likes to think he's from the ghetto,
but his middle class manners clash
with his manifesto.
He's rapping in an accent
that doesn't suit his hue.
Most of it is bollocks
and none of it is true!

So, what the fuck,
What the fuck,
What the fuck is he on about?

So, what the fuck,
What the fuck,
What the fuck is he on about?
So, what the fuck,
What the fuck,
What the fuck is he on about?

It's just random words in a random order,
random words in a random order.
Random words in a random order:
just put it down to an attention deficit disorder!

There's a woman on the stage;
though it's half an hour later,
she's still yet to make her point,
it would be kinder to sedate her.
Are we mocking the afflicted?
Yes we are!
Shouldn't everyone be free
to spout their raving rants regardless of the quality?
But what the fuck,
What the fuck,
What the fuck are they on about?
But what the fuck,
What the fuck,
What the fuck are they on about?
But what the fuck,
What the fuck,

What the fuck are they on about?
It's just random words in a random order,
random words in a random order.
Random words in a random order:
some people call it poetry but I just call it torture!
Random words in a random order.
Random words in a random order.
Random words in a random order.
as entertaining as a little kid with a recorder!

Believe What Thou Wilt

There are those who think the earth's a ball in orbit 'round the sun
and there are those who'll argue that the world is flat;
that it's rotating through degrees;
that the moon is made of cheese,
and there is nothing existential about that.
The world was built in seven days;
evolved over billions of years;
man was created as he stands before you now;
there are those whose claim is staked
that the dinosaurs were faked
and that nothing is more sacred than the cow.

Well…we would die to defy
any bigot that may try to deny you
the chance to air your views;
we'll lend our might to the fight
for your inalienable right
to believe whatever total bollocks you so choose.
We'd take up arms without qualms;
let them punch nails through our palms,
to protect whatever utter twaddle lights your fire;
we'd go to war to ensure
that your freedom will endure,
to trust whatever senseless drivel you desire.
There are those who spend their lives in preparation for the next
and some who follow a more hedonistic line.
Some people see conspiracy or can defend a monarchy
or throw their weight behind intelligent design.
There are those who think the universe revolves around themselves
or else some enigmatic psychopath they know or their children or their
dog or some old book t'which they're agog and the really mad ones just

go with the flow.

Well…we would die to defy

any bigot that may try to deny you

the chance to air your views;

we'll lend our might to the fight

for your inalienable right to believe whatever total bollocks you so choose.

We'd take up arms without qualms;

let them punch nails through our palms,

to protect whatever utter twaddle lights your fire.

We'd go to war to ensure that your freedom will endure, to trust whatever senseless drivel you desire.

There are cults, there are sects, there are movements and effects;

religions, covens, chapters, groups and clubs.

There are societies; sororities; the 'just- give-it-a-try' ities and people who just hang around in pubs.

But however they arrived at their decision to believe; whatever led the madman to his cause,

however fundamental or completely fuckin' mental:

their view's probably no crazier than yours!

Their view's probably no crazier than yours!

The Bards Of Bugger All

We are The Bards Of Bugger All:
The Bards Of Bugger All;
we're not sorry that we are not laureates
we are not waiting for your call.
We'll do it independently, apropo our philosophy.
We're entitled to go untitled
if that's the way we want to be.

We'd like to tell you what is on our minds;
what makes us seethe,
what troubles us; niggles and bugs us:
leaves us in a state of peeve.
We'd like to lay this on you;
open up and bare our souls
and we'll do it without ceremony;
pomp; fanfare or drum rolls.

'Cause we're The Bards Of Bugger All,
The Bards Of Bugger All;
we're applauded, but we're not lauded,
we've no pretensions that way at all.
We are not representative;
shun any epithets you'd give,
don't elevate us; celebrate with a fuss
and your children get to live!

We'll say our piece without concern for rules nor etiquette;
we'll walk the tightrope of good taste without a safety net.
You can listen or you can bugger off;
you can laugh; you can complain,
but we've no obligation to desist or to refrain.

We can say anything we like;
given a stage, an amp and a mic;
no king; no mayor; no throne-to-the heir
can impose their lyrical Reich,
so take y'queen's birthday honours farce
and y'keys to the city pass;
your knighthood; OBE shitehood:
you can shove 'em up your arse!

'Cause we're The Bards Of Bugger All,
yes, we're The Bards Of Bugger All;
we're not sorry that we are not laureates;
we're not waiting for that call.
We'll do it independently, apropo our philosophy.
We're entitled to go untitled
if that's the way we want to be.
'Cause we're The Bards Of Bugger All,
The Bards Of Bugger All;
we're applauded, but we're not lauded,
we've no pretensions that way at all.
We are not representative;
shun any epithets you'd give,
don't elevate us; celebrate with a fuss
and your children get to live!
Don't elevate us; celebrate with a fuss
and your children get to live!

Tights Not Stockings

I'm easily distracted by a pair of silky pins;
slinking down the high street go my curvy, shiny twins.
I try to keep a focus; I try not to be cock led,
by repeating this mantra over in my head:

(she's wearing)
Tights not stockings, tights not stockings,
tights not stockings, tights not stockings,
with a wire gauze gusset and a belt designed for locking.

They sidle past my window and I try to close my eyes,
but I'm imagining the friction on those sliding nylon thighs.
I'm waiting for a breeze to lift that little cotton skirt
and I'm hoping what I see there won't be bare and pink and pert!

Tights not stockings, tights not stockings,
tights not stockings, tights not stockings,
with a wire gauze gusset and a belt designed for locking.

They shimmer in the sunlight as they shimmy into view,
like a mirage in a desert that won't turn out to be true.
With all the allure of an oasis to a dehydrated man with a fetish for
suspenders and a depilation fan.

I wish I didn't waste so much time watching girls go by,
contemplating lacy lingerie in heels six inches high;
I've better things to do than lech'n leer'n fantasize:
I know what girls look like naked
so it won't be a surprise!

Tights not stockings, tights not stockings,
tights not stockings, tights not stockings,
with a wire gauze gusset and a belt designed for locking.

In A Poetocracy

We want to live in a poetocracy;
what we wouldn't give for a class and priv'lege free society;
that isn't a vain ideology:
we just think you'd be better off and
happier if things were left to the likes of we!

We've seen despots; ruthless dictators;
chinless, inbred runts with psychopathic tendencies,
all worming their way to the front.
We've had mad monarchs; pious bollocks,
masquerading as theocracy;
there can't be a man or a woman among us

who hasn't thought, 'is this the best it can be?'

We've seen off autocratic tyrants,
Who've told us how we ought to think;
imperialistic egotists who've taken the world to the brink.
We've had more than our share of fascist bully boy politos,
So surely it's time to ditch the system; bring in the poets and see how it
goes?

We want to live in a poetocracy;
what we wouldn't give for a class and priv'lege free society;
that's our philosophy and we're pretty sure you'd prefer it to this sham
of democracy.

In a free and fair election, we vote for the candidate of our choice from
a list that's been prepared for us we're led to believe we've a voice and
they've all been to Eton or Stowe, y'know: they're Bullingdon blue
blood elite, which makes 'em them prefect representatives for the

average bloke in the street!

We want to live in a poetocracy;
what we wouldn't give for a class and priv'lege free society;
that isn't a vain ideology:
we just think you'd be better off and
happier if things were left to the likes of we!

Soldier; policeman; MP: all jobs with a very big ask.
If you want to be any of these then you're not psychologic'ly up t'the
task.
It's a case of survival of the fittest; well, the richest, anyway: the law of
the corporate jungle keeps the working types at bay, but what about
thinkers and writers: the people who cogitate on?
Would they not be better suited leaders given their penchant for ranting
a wrong?

We want to live in a poetocracy;
what we wouldn't give for a class and priv'lege free society;
that isn't a vain ideology:
we just think you'd be better off and
happier if things were left to the likes of we!
We think you'd be better off and happier if things were left to the likes
of me.

I Like Girls

I'm not a man's man in any sense of the phrase;
I've never wanted to be that way.
Not into football or fighting or Friday night sluts or other ritualistic
macho displays.
And though I wear more makeup than some girls and my clothes may
look a little bit fey,
I've been told by the biggest queen I know,
that I don't cut a convincing gay!

I like girls,
'though I look a bit like one,
I like girls,
'though I look a bit queer,
I like girls
and I always have done,
so I'm sorry if you've had a bum steer.

I'm not a tran sexual/gender or vestite;
there's nothing swing about me that you might sway.
I'm not offended when you call me the campest straight guy
or a mincing, trolling old roué.
I'm comfortable with my sexuality and I don't give a shit what you say,
I've been told by the boys with the gaydar
that I don't cut a convincing gay.

I like girls,
'though I look a bit like one,
I like girls,
'though I look a bit queer,
I like girls
and I always have done,
so I'm sorry if you've had a bum steer...

Men Of A Muchness

We're both men of a muchness;
once upon a time we were the boys we're trying t'be,
but then we got old and a touch less
marketable as a teenage pop commodity.

So we suck in our bellies and we puff out our chest;
we sweep our hair a little higher and we pimp up the rest;
we add a little bit of shading and a smatter of gloss;
we're both in heels to aid our posture but we gather no moss.
We're on the wrong side of fifty so we don't hang about;
we still have lead in our pencils and a talent t'tout and so it takes a little
longer to get ready to serve,
but once we're going you will find we've still got stamina and verve.

We're both men of a muchness,
Once upon a time we were the boys we're trying t'be,
but then we got old and a touch less
marketable as a teenage pop commodity.

But now we're men of experience;
distinction and guile.
We've been there; seen it; done it, with impeccable style.
We've weathered the wars in pursuit of our arts;
you can tell our credentials from the scars on our hearts.
We bled our angst on the battlefields and lived t'tell tales;
swapped our innocence for wisdom:
freed our minds from their gaols.
The voice of youth has had its moment, but can never compare with
the savoir faire maturity of this seasoned pair.

We're both men of a muchness,

Once upon a time we were the boys we're trying t'be,
but then we got old and a touch less
marketable as a teenage pop commodity.
We're both men of a muchness,
We're both men of a muchness,
We're both men of a muchness,
We're both men of a muchness,
We're both men of a muchness,
We're both men of a muchness,
(repeat to fade)

Hanging With Poets

We've spent time in the company of thespians,
who dropped names with their ev'ry camp breath;
we've been anecdoted to distraction,
we were air-kissed and daaahlinked to death.
We've been out with clowns and with jesters;
all manics and miserable blokes,
and they bitched and they sniped at each other,
each the butt of the other man's jokes.
We indulged a band of rock minstrels;
we invited their egos to tea.
We pandered and pampered;
they primped, preened and tantrumed,
while admiring themselves on MTV.

So we're quaffing with wordsmiths and ranters;
we're imbibing with poets and bards,
we're wrapped in the presents of writers of the lyrical rebel vanguard.

We've known doctors and lawyers and self-made employers,
they've all shown us the world as they know it;
generals and bureaucrats spouting figures and facts,
but we'd much rather be hanging with poets.

Oh, we've heard statisticians and bent politicians say,
'this is the world as we know it';
we've been cleaned out by bankers and footballing wankers, so we'd
rather be hanging with poets.
Yes, we're broke, but we're hanging with poets;
we're broke because we're hanging with poets;
we're pissed 'cause we're hanging with poets.

Little Old Lady

She was a little old lady;
she lived through two world wars.
She was a little old lady;
fought with Pankhurst for the cause;
just a little old lady;
the neighbour everyone ignores,
'cause she smells of piss' n toffees
and wears wellingtons indoors.

'Come in and sit down, dear;
you're so kind to think of me.
There're some flapjacks in the biscuits tin;
I'll make a pot of tea.'
And she hobbled to the kitchen,
her back a shepherd's crook,
so riddled with arthritis, I could barely stand to look.
But she wouldn't let me help her,
though she looked so bent and frail,
she was just happy to have someone to listen to her tale.

She was a little old lady;
she lived through two world wars.
She was a little old lady;
fought with Pankhurst for the cause; just a little old lady;
the neighbour everyone ignores,
'cause she smells of cats and biscuits and wears rollers out of doors.

She hasn't had it easy;
she's a martyr to her pains.
She stiffens up in winter and get achy when it rains.
She's living in a tower block,
up fifteen flights of stairs;

she never had a family so there's no one else who cares.
But she goes to church on Sundays and she tends her husband's grave;
she's lonely and she's vulnerable,
but she tries to be so brave.

She was a little old lady;
she lived through two world wars.
She was a little old lady;
fought with Pankhurst for the cause;
just a little old lady;
the neighbour everyone ignores,
'cause she smells of fags and kippers and strains cabbage through her
drawers.

She was widowed in her twenties when her husband went to fight,
for freedom from fascism,
'cause he knew it wasn't right.
He died so future generations had the right to be safe from prejudice
and ideologically free,
but his sacrifice was wasted on his widow with her claim that
*'all these bloody foreigners comin' over her with their heathen religions and their dirty
foreign ways;*
*takin' our jobs; stealin' our 'ouses and shaggin' their way into our blood line: it ain't
right!*
That's who I blame!

Well…. She was a little old lady;
she lived through two world wars.
She was a little old lady;
fought with Pankhurst for the cause;
just a little old lady;
the neighbour everyone abhors,
'cause she smells of hate and mothballs and is Nazi to the core!

Champion The Underdog

There's a revolution cooking; I can feel it in me bones:
rebellion is brewing with anarchic undertones!
The silver spooned have had their way 'n say for long enough;
it's time to let the ordinaries strut their funky stuff,
because we're sick 'n tired of hearing about austerity,
where wages never rise unless you're an elected MP.
Whilst they cripple the middle with taxes to pay to clean their moats
and let billionaires off with a handshake if they promise to buy 'em
some votes!
But before you shout, 'incitement to riot', hear us out: the little man is
restless and he's rising to the shout of:
CHAMPION THE UNDERDOG!
CHAMPION THE UNDERDOG!

Now, I'm not suggesting violence;
this is not a call to arms,
nor to loot 'n burn our cities,
'cause it's only us that harms.
It's a silent insurrection:
a revolt within the law;
we need to turn their rules against them in a way they can't ignore.
A civilised sedition;
yeah: a middle class dissent;
insubordination from the lit'rate element!
We'll challenge and we'll conquer;
we'll play 'em at their game;
we'll buck the corporations and we'll do it our name!

The little man has spoken and his words are gaining clout,
gathering momentum as we join the shout of:
CHAMPION THE UNDERDOG!

CHAMPION THE UNDERDOG!

Draw out all your money and put it in a box,
that's fire, flood and rodent proof, with half a dozen locks.
Take that box and bury it, then watch the bankers stew,
with nothing left to gamble with and no one left to screw.
Boycott all the branded chains that we've let run amok, to strangle
competition and fix the price of stock.
Deny them their taxation,
try bartering or swap,
'cause that will stop them creaming their percentage off the top.

The little man is many and together we shall rout,
and without our contribution they may even shout out:
CHAMPION THE UNDERDOG!
CHAMPION THE UNDERDOG!

Pointy Dancing

He doesn't know the words,
but he will sing 'em anyway;
with a lager in each hand,
he'll stagger, totter, trip 'n sway.
He'll lurch around the dance floor like a zombified rhino;
he's that pissed bloke at your wedding that nobody seems to know...

They put her in a dress they thought would not outshine the bride;
she should've tried it on first 'cause she's falling out the side.
The rhythm's flowing through her as is all that sparkling wine,
she's that wankered maid-of-honour who's convinced she knows this line...

He's chatting up the bridesmaids;
he's giving it all that.
He thinks he's bagged the blonde one, but they both think he's a twat.
He's the best man they could hope for;
four ex-wives can't all be wrong.
He's dad-dancing like he's fitting, 'cause he thinks he knows this song...

Pointy dancing; pointy dancing:
what's with all the pointy dancing?
Every wedding that I go to its all finger jabbing prancing.
it's not a bloody football match;
all clenched salutes'n chanting:
dancing's s'posed to be erotic
and romantic mood enhancing.
Pointy dancing; pointy dancing:
what's with all the pointy dancing?
Every party that I go to it's just digit jousts'n lancing.
Where's the pogo or the polka;

no one's voguing or Prince Charming;
when did jigging round a handbag get aggressive and alarming?

The bride is in the flower bed; her arse is in the air.
Her g-string's ineffectual, but she's far too wazzed to care.
She was heading for the dance floor 'cause she heard her favourite
track; she's got guests to point 'n wail at whilst they point'n wail right
back…

Her old man's had to pay for it and its left him quite bereft;
it was s'posed t've been his pension fund, but now he's naff all left,
but he's finally got her out 'a the house and not a day too soon,
so he'll sing'n point with the rest of 'em;
the wrong words out of tune…

The vicar's in the corner;
she is piggin' out on cake.
She had a funeral before this and had trifle at the wake.
She had a tipple in the vestry, just to fortify her nerve,
now she's gesticulatin' from her pew with pious unreserve…

Pointy dancing; pointy dancing:
what's with all the pointy dancing?
Every wedding that I go to it's all finger jabbing prancing.
It's not a UKIP rally;
these aren't fascist hordes advancing,
it's a chav wedding reception,
they're not acid house rave trancing!

Pointy dancing; pointy dancing:
what's with all the pointy dancing?
Every party that I go to,
if that's dancing, I'm not asking,

where's the tango and the foxtrot that we used t'find entrancing?
If the lunge'n prod are a la mode,
then fuck off, I'm not chancing!

Pointy dance; pointy dance:
what's with the stupid pointy dance?
Don't point that finger my way or you'll need an ambulance!

Flesh'n Blood

Nobody is no one in the grand ol' scheme a'things;
we're all in this together,
whether paupers, queens or kings.
We all came through the same door;
we all end up in the mud,
so fuck yer airs'n graces, mate:
we're all just flesh'n blood.
You're 'aving a barf if you think we'll bow to you…

You want my respect;
you think we owe you more than you owe we;
you'd like us to defer t'your superiority.
T'tug our blessed forlocks;
doff our caps; avert our gaze:
prostrate ourselves afore ye;
kneel in subjugated praise.
Oh, just because you've strutted large on the international stage, or
published your opinions for us on the printed page;
just because you have a knack for something that we don't; we're not
obliged to idolise; don't expect us to:
We won't!
You're havin' a laugh if you think we'll bow to you…

Nobody is no one when it all comes tumblin' down;
the remnants of society won't fawn before a crown.
We're mostly made'a water;
we're all full of piss'n crud,
so fuck your airs'n graces, mate:
we're all just flesh'n blood.
You're 'av'n'a giraffe if you think we'll bow to you…

Oh look you've got a brand new car;
good lord, its four wheel drive,
with all mod con accoutrements to which you think we strive.
A nanny, you say and a cleaner;
a holiday home in Spain,
Well, this look is neither jealousy, resentment or disdain.
So, you're an actor! You're a singer! You're a TV game show host!
You model in your trollies,
you're the tip top toast!
In life, you were the bee's knees;
a cut above: the best,
but now you're six feet under,
you're as dead as all the rest.
You're 'av'n'a giraffe if you think we'll bow to you...

Nobody is no one when it's all said'n done:
everyone is equal underneath our shining sun.
There's nothing much between us in the naughty naked nud,
so fuck your airs'n graces, mate, we're all just flesh 'n blood.

Black, white, brown, yellow faces,
still, we're all just flesh'n blood
we come from different places,
but we're all still flesh'n blood.
The whole damned human race is only water, flesh'n blood.

Does My Bass

There's no easy way t'take it,
on a bike, he'd never make it,
and they'd never let him bring it on the bus,
if it had wheels, then we would ride it;
saddle up and sit astride it,
but I doubt it'd take the weight of the two of us.
Some have suggested we don't need it;
that's their view and we should heed it:
a normal bass guitar would easily suffice;
so much easier to manoeuvre it,
won't put your back out trying to move it,
well, that's as maybe,
but we're prepared to pay that price!

Edinburgh's cobbles,
they may shake it,
but there's no way we'd forsake it;
it's as much as part of us as him 'n me,
you would do well to remember,
it's a fully paid up member of the act
and as such: treated equally.
It can't walk because it lacks feet,
so we'll put it the back seat
of my car, then we'll open up the roof.
We'll wear hats because it's raining,
But don't think that we're complaining;
Just one question
And we'd like to know the truth…

Does my bass, (does my bass),
Does my bass, (does my bass),

Does my bass look good in this? x 4
It's got four strings that he can choose fr'm
and he's not afraid to use 'em,
whilst he's banging out the beat
behind the word,
it sets my lyric movin'
gives 'em life and gets 'em groovin',
that's the double bass to which I've previously referred!

I've seen poets who use drums,
cajons and bongos hit with thumbs;
guitars; pianos; harps and accordions;
ukuleles: tiny things,
but with the same amount of strings,
but which is better?
I'll ask the audience:

Does my bass, (does my bass),
Does my bass, (does my bass),
Does my bass look good in this? x 4

Umbrella Fair Northampton 2017 (Rosemarie Jarvis)

The Antipoet merchandise 2016

With Ed Tudor Pole at Poetry Cafe London 2010 (Ant Smith)

9. The Provenance Of The Beast…

"The only thing that can prepare you for The Antipoet is having seen them before"
—Wesley Freeman-Smith, Moving Tone, February 2013

In much the same way that journalists and biographers have been offering up the names of speculative fifth Beatles since the mid nineteen sixties, (was it Epstein, Sutcliffe, George Martin or Yoko Ono?) numerous have been the presumptions as to the identity of The Antipoet's mysterious 'Third Member'. Is it Donna: our fearless handler; without whom our rehearsal sessions would dissolve into alcohol infused slander spats before ever a rhyme could be mustered? No. Is it Mark 'Flash' Gordon, our peerless producer; the man who has devoted countless hours to making our recorded ravings palatable for the masses? No. Is it Steve Joy: musical polymath and master of disguise, who on occasion may be called upon to cover for one of us in times of dire emergency? No. Is it The Welsh Whisperer, Fay Roberts: bongo bothering parodist and most frequent of our regular stage crashers? No. Could it be 'Open Mic Ali'; without whose disdain for my poetry, this act might never have been created? Definitely not, no.

All would agree that there is one character that this story has so far all but ignored, yet without whose selfless devotion to our cause, you would not be reading this book! I'm referring, of course, to The Beast itself!

Often considered 'The Quiet One', due to his reluctance to partake in interviews and his need for a lie down immediately after a performance, The Beast's importance to this act; so often overlooked, can never be underestimated…

The Beast was created in Cremona, Italy in 1723; hand carved from the finest rosewood and inlaid with gilt by Stradivarius himself. It was to be one of his finest and also final masterful creations; a special commission for one of the most famous virtuosos of the age: Count Johann von Neumann; an Austrian wunderkind, renowned, not only for the speed and dexterity of the fingers of his left hand, but also for his enormous size, for Von Neumann was nothing short of a giant. Originally built as a huge violin, The Beast followed its master on a tour that was to take in every country, principality and territory of the time that was traversable by foot; striding across the land in his trademark top hat and high-heeled boots and dragging The Beast behind him strapped to a specially built handcart. Over the next twenty years the pair performed for kings, queens, maharajas and despotic, cannibalistic warlords alike; Stradivarius' most enigmatic instrument being heard in every corner of the globe and by an estimated ninety-nine percent of the population. It is believed to have rattled its way across more than twenty billion cobbles on its inaugural world tour; that's four whole cobbles more than in the entirety of Old Town Edinburgh!

But if there was one thing that Von Neumann was more famous for than his bowing and his plucking, it was his penchant for fiddling with the wives and daughters of rich and powerful men. It was hardly a surprise, then that his life would come to an abrupt and indignant end in single combat, on Hampstead Heath, in October, 1744.

On his death, The Beast's ownership, now a spoil of battle, transferred to the man who had bested him that day: the husband of a duchess whom the notorious maestro had been accused of knocking up.

For the cuckolded Duke, however, of whose identity history has failed to keep a definitive account, the outcome of this honour-restoring duel that foggy, autumnal morning was to be his final stroke of luck. For the bullet that pierced Von Neumann's heart that day, passed right through his body to wedge itself in the bejewelled neck of his oversized instrument; which had been leant against a tree directly behind him. It has been speculated that the Count's spirit passed with the shot, torn from his mortal carcass, to take up permanent spectral residence within the fabric of his pride and joy, from whence it could enact its bloody vengeance on its murderer, ensuring that

113

everything that the Duke touched from that point forward turned to shit.

An apocryphal tale? We'll probably never know for sure. What we do know, though, is that the Duke died a mysterious death a year to the day later when, whilst preparing to mount his maid from behind, bent over a trunk in the attic of his stately home, The Beast toppled from the shelf where it had been stashed, flattening him in the process. After that, it was deemed cursed by the family and was burned by the Duke's eldest son on a pyre in the grounds of their home.

The Duke's younger son, well, the boy whom he had brought up as his son, duly rescued it before it could be destroyed completely. He later recounted that he had heard it calling to him and had felt compelled to pull it from the flames, even though he lost both his hands to the inferno.

The Beast stayed with its rescuer for the rest of the man's life. Refusing to be parted from it, he took it with him wherever he went. A less cumbersome article by this point, owing to the fact that its head and neck had been completely burnt away in the fire, he had hinged the front piece, had a clasp and hasp added to it and had thus turned it into the chest in which he kept his belongings. He died in 1811 of persistent cock rot, passing his chattels to his own eldest son, who had been about to throw away his father's strange old chest when, in a dream, he'd heard it speaking to him. It had told him that he had to keep it in the family as, one day, it would become important and was destined to save the life of one of his distant progeny. And so the grandson, whose name was Jan, a man of meagre means, took it out into the garden, upended it and turned it into a chicken coop, where it stayed for the next twenty years. During this time it gradually began to deteriorate, a mixture of damp weather and chicken shit rotting its hand-carved planks, but Jan stubbornly refused to part with it, patching and repairing it regularly, panel by rotten panel. By the time that he too passed away, only the hinged front board remained of the original instrument.

It was inherited in 1836 by his only daughter, Dianne. On his deathbed her father had explained to her the importance of keeping it in the family, so Dianne broke up the coop, salvaged the last remaining piece of Johann von Neumann's original violin and set

114

about making it into a novelty occasional table.

It was on top of this table, some years later, that her cherry was popped by a wandering minstrel that she had taken a shine to and had invited back to her place for a post-gig shag. During said deflowering, the table broke in two and the conjugating pair found themselves entangled on the floor amongst the rubble. It was here, whilst pulling a rosewood splinter from Dianne's bare arse, that Ivan the wandering minstrel noticed some writing on the table's underside. In faded black ink it read: 'to my ol' mucka, Johann, best of luck—Stradivarius, August 1723'. Ivan recognised the signature immediately; authenticating it on the spot and with the aid of his thus impregnated new girlfriend, who was quite a renowned carpenter, as it went, set about restoring The Beast to its former glory.

The restoration project took them the remainder of their lives (she was good, but she was slow), with Ivan finally restringing the instrument on his deathbed in 1901.

The first person to play her since The Count, back in 1744, was to be his great, great grandson Iain Neumann, when it was handed to him at his parents' wake. Now, whether it was due to the fact that both his parents had been unwitting descendants of The Count himself or that he had been conceived on the body of the haunted violin itself or, possibly, a combination of all these factors, no one has ever been able to say, but the truth of the matter was that he had never played before. Mistaking it for a double bass, Iain immediately set about inventing the slapped style that is more commonly attributed to the psychobilly acts of the late fifties, yet his name seems also to have been left out of the annals of musical history.

Iain died an early and violent death in 1956, assassinated on stage, mid solo, in a New Orleans night club by a man whose wife the bassist had impregnated when his band had last been in town. In a weird case of history repeating itself, following his killer's subsequent execution, Iain's bass was inherited by the daughter that he'd never even known he had, an American by the name of Diaphonean. It was Diaphonean who replaced the original Stradivarian, rosewood sound board, which had a double-barrelled hole in it, with a chipboard alternative to match the rest of its panels. It was varnished

115

and became famous all over again as the 'house bass' at the jazz club that she subsequently opened in her late father's name.

In 2009, I mentioned to my new poeting partner, Jan, that the acquisition of a double bass might be the making of our act. A quick flick through ebay later and The Beast again became the property of a Von Neumann descendant.

'I can't play double bass, though,' the great, great, great, great, grandson of the instrument's first owner bemoaned.

'I wouldn't worry,' I remarked, 'for £550 I'd imagine it comes pre-haunted by its original owner.'

And you know what, it was!

"You guys ROCKSTARRED the place… woooo… ENCORE!"
—Huw Dylan Elilis, Nozstock Festival, July 2011

Warming up for Adam Ant at the Watford Colloseum 2017 (Mark Ward)

10. Were You There? (Gig list 2008 to 2017)

"Combining music, poetry and comedy is one of the hardest things to pull off, but they do it brilliantly."
—Paul Lyalls, August 2010

2008

Summer of:
began rehearsing a covers set together (comprising of Ian Dury, Adam Ant and Tenpole Tudor songs) and performing them at the Flint Cottage open mic in High Wycombe every other Thursday.

December:
wrote our first two originals 'This Is Me' and 'I Am The Antipoet'...

2009

8/1 (First gig as The Antipoet) The Flint Cottage, High Wycome.
15/1 (First RRRANTS) The Poetry Cafe, Covent Garden.
22/1 The Swan open mic, Beaconsfield.
4/2 The Horns open mic, Watford.
12/2 The Sportsman open mic, Croxley Green.
18/2 The Horns open mic, Watford.
12/3 The Sportsman open mic, Croxley Green.
24/3 RRRANTS at The Bell, Prince's Risborough.
31/3 The Pump House open mic, Watford.
13/4 Misfits, Hoxton.
22/4 Oral Cabaret, St Albans.
30/4 The Glasshouse open mic, High Wycome.
4/5 The Fox & Hounds, Rickmansworth.

6/5 The Horns open mic, Watford.

10/5 RRRANTS at The Horns, Watford.

6/6 Beaconsfield Lit Fest

7/6 RRRANTS at The Horns, Watford.

24/6 RRRANTS at Watford Library.

11/6 RRRANTS at The Poetry Cafe, Covent Garden.

12/6 The Horns open mic, Watford.

12/6 RRRANTS at Music On The Moor Festival, Hemel Hempstead.

18/6 an empty shop in the Eden centre, High Wycombe.

29/6 RRRANTS at Watford Library.

2/8 open mic, Chesham Football Club.

5/8 RRRANTS at The Horns, Watford.

9/8 The Horns open mic, Watford.

9/8 open mic, Chesham Football Club.

24-27/8 The Edinburgh Fringe: various open mics and busking stages.

8/9 RRRANTS at The Goat, St Albans.

13/9 RRRANTS at The Horns, Watford.

23/9 Oral Cabaret, St Albans.

25/9 RRRANTS at The White Hart Hotel, St Albans.

30/9 The Horns open mic, Watford.

8/9 Wendover Library.

11/9 open mic at Chesham Football Club.

16/9 RRRANTS at The Poetry Cafe, Covent Garden.

23/10 The Flint Cottage open mic in High Wycombe.

29/10 'Rhyme & Reason' book launch, Beaconsfield.

8/11 RRRANTS at The Horns, Watford.

12/11 RRRANTS at Watford Library.

17/11 RRRANTS at The Goat, St Albans.

22/11 open mic at Chesham Football Club.

24/11 Speech Motion, Shoreditch.

25/11 Free Speech, Cha Cha Cha, Watford.

8/12 RRRANTS at The Camden Eye.

11/12 RRRANTS at Watford Library.

2010

10/1 Tongue In Cheek, Wolverton.

19/1 RRRANTS at The Goat, St Albans.

21/1 The Hopbine open mic, Cambridge.

28/1 RRRANTS at Etcetera, Camden (with TV SMITH).

31/1 RRRANTS at The Camden Eye.

1/2 The Cock, Sarratt.

4/2 The Cross Kings, Kings Cross.

6/2 The Fox & Hounds, Rickmansworth.

9/2 Scribal Gathering, Stony Stratford.

11/2 Bang Said The Gun, Borough.

17/2 RRRANTS at The Poetry Cafe, Covent Garden.

6/3 The White Bear, Rickmansworth, open mic.

7/3 RRRANTS at The Camden Eye.

9/3 Scribal Gathering, Stony Stratford.

14/3 Tongue In Cheek, Wolverton.

25/3 a narrow boat on the Grand Union Canal, Cowley.

26/3 open mic at Chesham Football Club.

30/3 RRRANTS at The Goat, St Albans.

9/4 Poetry Kapow! Wolverton.

18/4 RRRANTS at The Camden Eye.

20/4 REEL REBELS RADIO INTERVIEW.

29/4 RRRANTS at The Olde Kings Arms, Hemel Hempstead.

6/5 Words & Music In The Woods, Muswell Hill.

13/5 Bang Said The Gun, Borough.

15, 16/5 RRRANTS at Rickmansworth Canal Festival.

19/5 RRRANTS at The Poetry Cafe, Covent Garden.

27/5 RRRANTS at The Olde Kings Arms, Hemel Hempstead.

31/5 Owlsworld at The Cock, Sarratt.

1/6 RRRANTS at The Goat, St Albans.

13/6 RRRANTS at The Camden Eye.

16/6 Raising The Awen, Northampton.

20/6 The Waterside Festival, Milton Keynes. (launch of TIGHTS NOT STOCKINGS).

21/6 Norwich Arts Centre.

22/6 Ruislip High School.

22/6 Cha Cha Cha, Watford.

23/6 The Brewery Tap, Peterborough.

27/6 RRRANTS at St Albans busking festival.

14/7 Hammer & Tongue, Oxford.

15/7 RRRANTS at The Olde Kings Arms, Hemel Hempstead.

16, 17/7 Larmer Tree Festival, Shaftsbury.

18/7 The Buxton Fringe.

21/7 RRRANTS at The Poetry Cafe, Covent Garden (with ED TUDORPOLE).

22/7 Bang Said The Gun, Borough.

23/7 Poetry Kapow! Wolverton.

27/7 RRRANTS at The Goat, St Albans.

6,7,8,9/8 RRRANTS Ranting Festival at The Camden Eye (with VIV ALBERTINE & HELEN McCOOKERYBOOK & DEN HEGARTY).

30/8 Zenith Bar, Angel.

2/9 Words & Music In The Woods, Muswell Hill.

7/9 RRRANTS at The Goat, St Albans.

16/9 Poets On Fire, Lewes.

20/9 Norwich Arts Centre.

26/9 RRRANTS at The Camden Eye.

30/9 RRRANTS at The Olde Kings Arms, Hemel Hempstead.

2/10 The Limelight open mic, Aylesbury.

7/10 RRRANTS at The Camden Eye.

12/10 RRRANTS at The Goat, St Albans.

15/10 Poetry Kapow, Wolverton.

20/10 Raising The Awen, Northampton.

27/10 The Adelaide, Teddington.

31/10 RRRANTS at The Camden Eye.

2/11 Speechmotion, Camden.

3/11 Monkey Kettle, Milton Keynes.

6/11 Slam Final, Wolverhampton.

11/11 RRRANTS at The Olde Kings Arms, Hemel Hempstead.

14/11 The Teabox, Richmond.

17/11 RRRANTS at The Camden Eye (ATILLA!).

20/11 George & Carrie's wedding, Welwyn.

23/11 Cha Cha Cha, Watford.

24/11 The Adelaide, Teddington.

28/11 Tongue In Cheek, Wolverton.

8/12 RRRANTS at The Horns, Watford.

9/12 The Urban Bar, Whitechapel.

11, 12/12 RRRANTS at The Camden Eye.

14/12 London Bridge.

15/12 RRRANTS at The Queen's Head, Chesham.

21/12 RRRANTS at The Goat, St Albans.

23/12 Quirkey at The Victoria, Dalston.

2011

2/1 RRRANTS at The Camden Eye.

13/1 The Sportsman, Croxley Green.

18/1 Cha Cha Cha, Watford.

20/1 RRRANTS at The Olde Kings Arms, Hemel Hempstead.

31/1 The Emperor, Cambridge.

3/2 Words & Music In The Woods, Muswell Hill.

6/2 RRRANTS at The Camden Eye.

8/2 Scribal Gathering, Stony Stratford.

11/2 The Teabox, Richmond.

15/2 RRRANTS at The Goat, St Albans.

17/2 Bang Said The Gun, Borough.

18/2 Poetry Kapow, Wolverton.

1/3 RRRANTS at OVO, St Albans.

6/3 RRRANTS at The Camden Eye.

8/3 Catweazle, Kilburn.

11/3 a dingy basement in Hackney.

12/3 Vegibite, Hove (HEATHER MILLS McCARTNEY)

15/3 RRRANTS at The Emperor, Cambridge.

17/3 RRRANTS at The Olde Kings Arms, Hemel Hempstead.

22/3 RRRANTS at OVO, St Albans.

30/3 The Word Cafe, Teddington.

1/4 The Fiddler's Elbow, Camden.

3/4 RRRANTS at The Camden Eye.

6/4 RRRANTS at The Queen's Head, Chesham.

14/4 RRRANTS at The Camden Eye.

26/4 RRRANTS at The Goat, St Albans.

1/5 The Camden Crawl

1/5 RRRANTS at The Camden Eye.

6/5 Waterside, Newport Pagnell.

8/5 Hideaway, Archway.

10/5 Scribal Gathering, Stony Stratford.

12/5 RRRANTS at OVO, St Albans.

17/5 RRRANTS at The Horns, Watford.

21, 22/5 RRRANTS at Rickmansworth Canal Festival.

28/5 Meadowlands Festival, Glynde.

7/6 Stony Live, Stony Stratford.

9/6 Bang Said The Gun, Borough.

11/6 The Wilmington, Clerkenwell.

14/6 RRRANTS at The Goat, St Albans.

19/6 Waterside Festival, Milton Keynes.

25/6 Watford Market.

3/7 RRRANTS at The Camden Eye.

8/7 Ledbury Poetry Festival.

9/7 The Grand Prix, Silverstone.

10/7 RRRANTS at Music On The Moor Festival, Hemel Hempstead.

18/7 Amici, Croxley Green.

20/7 Hammer & Tongue, Cambridge.

22, 23, 24/7 RRRANTS at The Camden Eye.

30, 31/7 Nozstock Festival, Hereford.

5/8 The Quirky.

7/8 RRRANTS at The Camden Eye.

9/8 RRRANTS at The Horns, Watford.

21-28/8 The Peartree, Edinburgh Fringe.

3/9 Watford Market.

4/9 RRRANTS at The Camden Eye.

14/9 Spoonful Of Poison, Stoke Newington.

16/9 The Teabox, Richmond.

17/9 The Imperial, Bilston.

23/9 The Teabox, Richmond.

28/9 Sage & Time, Holborn.

2/10 RRRANTS at The Camden Eye.

9/10 George's Book Launch, Hemel Hempstead.

11/10 Scribal Gathering, Stony Stratford.

13/10 Reading Comedy Festival.

18/10 RRRANTS at The Goat, St Albans.

26/10 The Word Cafe, Teddington.

1/11 Dyspla, Camden

5/11 Dyspla, Camden

6/11 RRRANTS at The Camden Eye.

13/11 RRRANTS at The Horns, Watford.

17/11 Bang Said The Gun, Borough.

26/11 Liverpool Town Hall.

4/12 RRRANTS at The Camden Eye.

11/12 Viva, Bristol.

14/12 Waterside, Newport Pagnell.

20/12 RRRANTS at The Goat, St Albans.

30/12 The Half Moon, Herne Hill.

2012

9/1 The Cross Kings, Kings Cross.
17/1 RRRANTS at The Goat, St Albans.
21/1 BARDAID BOOK SIGNING, WATERSTONES, HEMEL HEMPSTEAD.
22/1 RRRANTS at The Camden Eye.
29/1 Speechmotion, Shoreditch.
31/1 Scribal Gathering, Stony Stratford.
5/2 RRRANTS at The Camden Eye.
7/2 The Red Lion, High Wycombe.
11/2 The Watershed, Newport Pagnell.
12/2 The Sportsman, Croxley Green.
14/2 Scribal Gathering, Stony Stratford.
16/2 90th birthday soiree, Maida Vale.
19/2 RRRANTS at The Horns, Watford.
27/2 a shop window, Teddington.
1/3 BANG TV PILOT RECORDING.
4/3 RRRANTS at The Camden Eye.
7/3 Kiss The Sky, Hampstead.
13/3 RRRANTS at The Goat, St Albans.
18/3 Ely Festival.
18/3 Morgan's Wine Bar, Leighton Buzzard.
21/3 Raising The Awen, Northampton.
31/3 The Flag, Watford.
1/4 RRRANTS at The Camden Eye.
3/4 The Four Kings open mic, Dunstable.
8/4 The Kings Arms, Waterloo.
15/4 Wenlock Literary Festival.
24/4 RRRANTS at The Goat, St Albans.
27/4 Roman Fields School, Boxmoor.
1/5 Bar Des Arts, Guildford.

6/5 RRRANTS at The Camden Eye.

7/5 Queen's Wood Festival, Muswell Hill.

12, 13, 14/5 The Brighton Festival.

13/5 The Signalman open mic, Brighton.

19, 20/5 RRRANTS at The Rickmansworth Festival.

20/5 RRRANTS at The Horns, Watford.

2/6 The 100 Club, London.

3/6 Meadowlands Festival, Glynde.

3/6 RRRANTS at The Camden Eye.

4/6 street party, Teddington.

7/6 Scribal Gathering, Stony Stratford.

12/6 RRRANTS at The Goat, St Albans.

16/6 Waterside Festival, Milton Keynes.

30/6 Ryan's Bar, Stoke Newington.

30/6 Oxford Fire station.

1/7 RRRANTS at The Camden Eye.

13/7 Paper Tiger, Vauxhall.

17/7 RRRANTS at The Goat, St Albans.

22/7 Allographic, Cambridge.

28/7 Watford Market.

28/7 Paul's Mum'n Dad's Party, Croxley Green.

29/7 The Bardic Picnic, Northampton.

29/7 World Picnic, Milton Keynes.

4/8 Pippa & Vinnie's wedding, Basildon.

9/8 The Goat, St Albans.

11/8 Watford Market.

18/8 The Hat Factory, Luton.

19/8 RRRANTS at The Horns, Watford.

22/8 RRRANTS at The Leather Bottle, Leverstock Green.

26/8 The Kings Arms, Waterloo.

1/9 The Pembroke Castle, Camden.

2/9 RRRANTS at The Camden Eye.

9/9 The Bandstand, Hemel Hempstead.

18/9 RRRANTS at The Goat, St Albans.

4/10 The Dogstar, Brixton.

5/10 Reading Comedy Festival.

7/10 RRRANTS at The Camden Eye.

10/10 RRRANTS at The Leather Bottle, Leverstock Green.

11/10 RRRANTS at The Roxy, Borough.

12/10 The Maltings, St Albans.

19/10 The Teabox, Richmond.

20/10 Watford Bowls Club, Woodside.

23/10 RRRANTS at The Goat, St Albans.

27/10 Wycombe Arts Centre.

3/11 The Drawing Room, Chesham.

4/11 RRRANTS at The Camden Eye.

7/11 Friggers Of Speech, Crouch End.

8/11 RRRANTS at The Roxy, Borough.

13/11 Scribal Gathering, Stony Stratford.

14/11 RRRANTS at The Leather Bottle, Leverstock Green.

15/11 Suffolk University, Ipswich.

17/11 Tring.

18/11 RRRANTS at The Horns, Watford.

25/11 Kings Arms, Waterloo.

1/12 Stony Stratford Library.

2/12 The Bandstand, Hemel Hempstead.

4/2 Filthy McNasty's, Angel.

4/2 Wycombe University.

12/12 RRRANTS at The Leather Bottle, Leverstock Green.

16/12 The Bandstand, Hemel Hempstead.

17/12 Boogaloo, Highgate.

18/12 RRRANTS at The Goat, St Albans.

2013

6/1 RRRANTS at The Camden Eye.

8/1 Kidderminster.

17/1 Bang Said The Gun, Borough.

22/1 The Bardic Trials, Stony Stratford.

24/1 RRRANTS at The Roxy, Borough.

29/1 Bar Des Arts, Guildford.

4/2 RRRANTS at The Camden Head.

8/2 The Teahouse, Vauxhall.

11/2 The Greennote, Camden.

12/2 Scribal Gathering, Stony Stratford.

16/2 The Word Cafe, Teddington.

17/2 The Fountain, Cambridge.

19/2 RRRANTS at The Goat, St Albans.

27/2 Express Excess, Camden.

4/3 RRRANTS at The Camden Head.

10/3 The Finsbury, Finsbury Park.

11/3 The Sozzled Sausage, Lemington Spa.

24/3 RRRANTS at The Horns, Watford.

1/4 RRRANTS at The Camden Head.

10/4 Friggers Of Speech, Crouch End.

17/4 Raising The Awen, Northampton.

6/5 RRRANTS at The Camden Head.

14/5 RRRANTS at The Goat, St Albans.

18/5 Rickmansworth Festival.

22/5 Pearshaped, Fitzrovia.

24/5 The Concorde Club, Cranford.

31/5 Brighton Festival.

1/6 Strawberry Fayre, Cambridge.

1, 2/6 Brighton Festival.

3/6 RRRANTS at The Camden Head.

26/6 The Attic, Hackney.

27,28,29,30/6 GLASTONBURY. (X5)

1/7 RRRANTS at The Camden Head.

3/7 Words & Music In The Woods, Muswell Hill.

11/7 Apples & Snakes, Plymouth.
12/7 The Aston Clinton Beer Festival.
20/7 Larmer Tree Festival (x4)
23/7 RRRANTS at The Goat, St Albans.
4/8 The Bardic Picnic, Northampton.
17-25/7 The Edinburgh Fringe (x19)
26/8 Blythe Power Ashes, Peterborough.
2/9 RRRANTS at The Camden Head.
12/9 RRRANTS at Coco, Croxley Green.
13/9 Scribal Gathering, Stony Stratford.
14/9 The Alarmist magazine launch, WC1.
15/9 RRRANTS at The The Horns, Watford.
7/10 RRRANTS at The Camden Head.
8/10 RRRANTS at Scribal Gathering, Stony Stratford.
11/10 The Firefly, Oxford.
22/10 RRRANTS at The Goat, St Albans.
30/10 Raising The Awen, Northampton.
6/11 The Dashwood Arms, West Wycombe.
14/11 RRRANTS at Coco, Croxley Green.
17/11 RRRANTS at The Horns, Watford.
2/12 RRRANTS at The Camden Head.
5/12 The Word Cafe, Teddington.
8/12 The Lexington, Kings Cross.
15/12 Boogaloo, Highgate.
17/12 RRRANTS at The Goat, St Albans.

2014

6/1 RRRANTS at The Camden Head.
10/1 Wingrave Golf Club.
21/1 The Bardic Trials, Stony Stratford.
1/2 The Limelight, Aylesbury.
2/2 The Pleasance, Islington.

3/2 RRRANTS at The Camden Head.
6/2 The Comedy Cafe, Shoreditch.
11/2 Scribal Gathering, Stony Stratford.
25/2 RRRANTS at The Goat, St Albans.
3/3 RRRANTS at The Camden Head.
22/3 Raising The Awen, Northampton.
23/3 The Finsbury, Finsbury Park.
5/4 The Limelight, Aylesbury.
7/4 RRRANTS at The Camden Head.
12/4 Chat's Palace, Hackney.
13/4 The Pleasance, Islington.
14/4 The Lamb, Surbiton.
29/4 RRRANTS at The Goat, St Albans.
4/5 The Kings Arms, Waterloo.
5/5 RRRANTS at The Camden Head.
7/5 FUBAR RADIO SESSION AND INTERVIEW.
17/5 Yorkie Fest, Stony Stratford.
17/5 RRRANTS at The Rickmansworth Festival.
20/5 Bar Des Arts, Guildford.
29/5 Rose Theatre, Twickenham.
2/6 RRRANTS at The Camden Head.
5/6 Words & Music In The Woods, Muswell Hill.
7/6 Strawberry Fair, Cambridge.
7/6 Stony Live Festival, Stony Stratford.
8/6 Crouch End Fesival.
11/6 RRRANTS at Coco, Croxley Green.
12/6 Scribal Gathering, Stony Stratford.
21/6 Waterside Festival, Milton Keynes.
24/6 RRRANTS at The Goat, St Albans.
26/6 Glastonbury (x10)
17/7 The Magnolia Club, High Wycombe.
19/7 Larmer Tree Festival, Shaftsbury (x4)
25/7 Aston Clinton Beer Festival.

130

31/7 Twickenham.

6/8 The Boot, St Albans.

9/8 Scribal Gathering, Stony Stratford.

15,17/8 The Camden Fringe.

22/8 Blythe Power Ashes, Peterborough.

31/8 The Bardic Picnic, Northampton.

1/9 RRRANTS at The Camden Head.

9/9 The Keystone, Guildford.

13/9 Watford Museum.

14/9 Ham & High Litfest, Hampstead.

21/9 London Colney.

26/9 Marsworth Comedy Festival.

4/10 Mine Sweeper, Deptford.

5/10 Sunday Assembly,WC1.

6/10 RRRANTS at The Camden Head.

14/10 Scribal Gathering, Stony Stratford.

17/10 York House, Stony Stratford.

25/10 RRRANTS at Coco, Croxley Green.

29/10 Raising The Awen, Northampton.

3/11 RRRANTS at The Camden Head.

5/11 The Lamb, Surbiton.

12/11 RRRANTS at Coco, Croxley Green.

15/11 Watford Museum.

24/11 Surrey Writers.

29/11 Stony Stratford library.

1/12 RRRANTS at The Camden Head.

15/12 Boogaloo, Highgate.

23/12 The Boot St Albans.

2015

7/1 The Dashwood Arms, West Wycombe.

17/1 The Oak, Aston Clinton.

25/1 RRRANTS at Coco, Croxley Green.
27/1 The Bardic Trials, Stony Stratford.
1/2 Stoke Newington.
5/2 Bang Said The Gun, Borough.
10/2 Scribal Gathering, Stony Stratford.
20/2 Hunt Saboteurs Benefit, Northampton.
23/2 FUBAR RADIO: SESSION & INTERVIEW
28/2 FUBAR RADIO: LIVE.
2/3 The Keystone, Guildford.
11/3 Friggers Of Speech, Crouch End.
26/3 The Bus Driver's Prayer, Shoreditch.
29/3 RRRANTS at Coco, Croxley Green.
18/4 Community Centre, Hitchin.
19/4 Trestle Arts, St Albans.
16/5 Yorkie Fest, Stony Stratford.
16/5 RRRANTS at The Rickmansworth Festival.
30/5 Trestle Arts, St Albans.
31/5 RRRANTS at Coco, Croxley Green.
4/6 Utter, Luton.
6/6 Boxmoor Golf Club.
10/6 Friggers Of Speech, Crouch End.
20/6 Marsworth Festival.
22/6 The Betsy Trotwood, Farringdon.
24/6 Glastonbury (x15).
4/7 Woodoaks Farm, Maple Cross.
8/7 The Boot, St Albans.
16/7 The Larmer Tree Festival, Shaftsbury (x3)
19/7 Citadel Festival, Hackney.
31/7 Aston Clinton Beer Festival.
9-12/8 Edinburgh Fringe (x5).
29/8 Blythe Power Ashes, Tewkesbury.
30/8 Wycombe Fest.
9/9 The Boot, St Albans.

13/9 The Bridges, Ratlinghope.

19/9 Jon and Jill's wedding, Stony Stratford.

21/9 Boogaloo, Highgate.

3/10 Trestle, St Albans

13/10 Scribal Gathering, Stony Stratford.

21/10 Friggers at The Blighty, Finsbury Park.

24/10 Warriors Assemble, Newport.

25/10 RRRANTS at Coco, Croxley Green.

28/10 The Boot, St Albans.

31/10 Trestle Arts, St Albans.

1/11 The Garibaldi, St Albans.

10/11 The Olde Firestation, Oxford,

25/11 The Boot, St Albans.

28/11 Stony Stratford library.

6/12 RRRANTS at Coco, Croxley Green.

17/12 RRRANTS at Coco, Croxley Green.

21/12 Boogaloo, Highgate.

2016

1/1 St Albans Swimming Pool.

9/2 Scribal Gathering, Stony Stratford.

16/2 Allographic, Cambridge.

21/2 Nursing home, Radlett.

23/2 Black's Club, Soho.

16/3 Scribal Gathering, Stony Stratford.

18/3 NN1, Northampton.

31/3 Youth Hostel, Hemel Hempstead.

1/4 The Junction, Cambridge.

5/4 The Book Club, Hackney.

6/4 Small Horse Inn, Bristol.

7/4 Komedia, Brighton.

12/4 The Old Fire Station, Oxford.

13/4 Horse & Stables, Waterloo.
24/4 RRRANTS at Coco, Croxley.
30/4 Trestle Arts, St Albans.
15/5 The Devonshire Arms, Cambridge.
21/5 RRRANTS at The Rickmansworth Festival.
4/6 Strawberry Fair, Cambridge (x3).
5/6 Glastonwick, Brighton.
7/6 York House, Stony Stratford.
15/6 Raising The Awen, Northampton.
17/6 The Farmer's Boy, Kensworth.
18/6 Worcestershire LitFest & Fringe.
23-26/6 Glastonbury (x7).
4/7 The Horns, Watford.
14-16/7 Larmer Tree Festival, Shaftsbury (x4).
21/7 The Cabbage Patch, Twickenham.
29/7 Camp Bestival, Lulworth Cove.
5-7/8 Green Gathering, Chepstow (x6).
14/8 Wed Fest, Lewes.
21/8 Umbrella Fair, Northampton (x2).
27/8 Wed Fest, Kettering.
28/8 Blythe Power Ashes, Tewkesbury.
29/8 Small World Festival, Ashford.
7/9 Rodells, Watford.
15/9 The Vaults, Stony Stratford.
17/9 Worcester Music Festival.
25/9 Rec Rock Fest, Buxworth.
1/10 Shindig, Yeovil.
19/10 Raising The Awen, Northampton.
29/10 Animal Antiks Video shoot, Stoke Mandeville.
30/10 Perch, Croxley Green.
18/10 Hoxton.
7/12 Science seminar, Manchester.
9/12 Hemel Football Club.
134

12/12 The Water Rats, Kings Cross.

18th Perch, Croxley Green.

28th Hare & Hounds, St Albans.

2017

25/3 Tony's Dojo, Coventry.

31/3 The Farmer's Boy, Kensworth.

12/4 The Cock Hotel, Stony Stratford.

20/5 RRRANTS at The Rickmansworth Festival.

24/5 The Colosseum, Watford (ADAM ANT).

1/6 Micklefield Hall, Sarratt.

3/6 Strawberry Fair, Cambridge.

14/6 42Worcester Special—Worcestershire LitFest & Fringe.

16/6 Raconteurs, at The Trades, Hebden Bridge.

18/6 In Other Words Festival, Cambridge.

22-25/6 Glastonbury (x12)

23/7 RRRANTS at Perch, Croxley Green.

3/8 Rebellion, Blackpool (TOYAH).

5/8 Green Gathering, Chepstow.

12/8 Lakes Festival, Ledbury.

20/8 Umbrella Fair, Northampton.

27/8 Blythe Ashes, Tewkesbury.

31/8 The Three Cocks, Kettering.

1/9 Tiki, Hemel Hempstead.

2/9 Jo and Ruth's wedding, Malvern.

8/9 Bestival, Lulworth Cove.

14/9 Vaultage, Stony Stratford.

23/9 Fort William, Scotland.

12/11 The Queens Head, Long Marston.

29/11 The Jericho,Oxford

3/12 The ElmTree, Cambridge

11/12 Southampton University

12/12 Scribal Gathering Stony Stratford
28/12 The Horns, Watford

To date: 649 gigs

> **"Great material! Totally professional but completely unpretentious."**
> —Jude Simpson, August 2010

11. Thank You's

"You guys built a vibe. Did it for me big time."
—David J, August 2010

Paul & Ian would like to thank the following people for their help during their first ten years:

Donna Ray Daniels-Moss (obviously); Emma Sparre-Slater, Mark Gordon; Simon Wilson; Steve Joy; Ali Curry; Paul Solomons; Jonathon Lambton; Jo Bell; Helen & Benita Johnson; Emma Chesterton; Vicky Laxton-Bass; Poeterry; Mark Niel; Graeme Edgar of vponline and FUBAR Radio.

And far too many individuals to mention by name, but you know who you are, you lovely people!

12. About The Author

In 1984 a journalist writing for The Watford Observer dubbed 'wannabe enigmatic pop star' Paul 'Eccentric' because he refused to give his surname during an interview. It stuck. For the past thirty years he has been writing, directing and performing under this ridiculous moniker, but at least it got him noticed.

He is a published songwriter, poet, playwright and novelist.

His debut novel, *Down Among The Ordinaries* was published by United Press in 2004. He then spent the next few years writing and directing for stage and radio, which culminated in his first Edinburgh Fringe run with his play *The Sorry People*.

In 2009, along with Ian Newman and Donna Daniels-Moss, Paul co-founded **Rhythmical Ravings and Rants** (RRRANTS), a poetry, song writing, comedy and storytelling collective. Their first in-house publication was Paul's poetry collection; *The Kult Of The Kazoo* at the end of 2009.

In 2010 he published a self-help guide to performing, based on his performance workshops and coaching classes entitled *Quaking In Me Stackheels*. He followed this in 2013 with *Rrrantanory Little Stories*, a collection of bedtime stories for adults; both for Desert Hearts Publishing. In 2015 he wrote, *The Edinburgh Fringe In A Nutshell* which was published by Burning Eye Books; a guide to taking your first show to the biggest arts festival in the world.

He has written numerous plays and stories as well as documentaries and articles for radio and has had his poetry featured in various newspapers, magazines and anthology books.

He is probably best known as the mouthy half of dyslexic poetry duo 'The Antipoet': the beatrantin' rhythm'n views act that currently takes up most of his life.

He has been fronting The Odd Eccentric since 1984, albeit with a break during the mid 1990s, and The Senti-Mentals on and off since 1996, along with several other bands: Polkabilly Circus, Sly Quip & The

Quickwits, SLOB and The Rocketeers.

When not writing or performing he is Artistic Director, and one third of the triumvirate behind The RRRANTS Collective, helping to promote and disseminate independent poets, songwriters and storytellers. He is available for compering duties, events hosting and after-dinner speaking if you're very, very brave.

His passions include The BARDAID Initiative (of which he is the founder), Doctor Who, vegetable growing, punk rock, animals, the countryside and Donna.

He has no truck with bigots, nazis, supermarkets, the gentry, and animal killers.

He is a committed anarchist, atheist and vegetarian and a keeper of cats, ducks, goats and chickens and continues to sponsor various donkeys, sheep, dogs, llamas and most recently a herd of reindeer.

He lives with his wife, Donna, in Aston Clinton, Buckinghamshire.

Paul Eccentric – Publications List

Lyrical Quibble and Quip (2001) Published by JOKAT Audio
ISBN 978-0-9555340-2-7
The Periphrast (2002) Published by JOKAT Audio
ISBN 978-0-9555340-0-3
Out Of The Frying Pan (2003) Published by JOKAT Audio 2003
ISBN 978-0-9555340-1-0
Down among The Ordinaries (2004) Published by United Press
ISBN 1-84436-092-X
The Kult of The Kazoo (2009) Published by RRRANTS Publishing
ISBN 978-0-9555340-3-4
Quaking in Me Stackheels (2010) Published by DesertHearts
ISBN 978-1-898948-97-1
Rrrantanory CDs (2011) Published by RRRANTS Publishing Series 1
ISBN 978-0-9555340-9-6
Rrrantanory CDs (2012) Published by RRRANTS Publishing Series 2
ISBN 978-0-9572808-2-3
Rrrantanory CDs (2013) Published by RRRANTS Publishing Series 3
ISBN 978-0-9572808-4-7
Rrrantanory Little Stories (2013) Published by DesertHearts
ISBN 978-1-908755-07-0
The Edinburgh Fringe In A Nutshell (2015) Published by Burning Eye
Books
ISBN 9-781909-136564

'Rant-Along-An-Antipoet' DVD Credits...

All tracks written and performed by The Antipoet (Paul Eccentric & Ian Newman); cameras operated by Jonathon Taylor & Emma Sparre-Slater; edited by Ian Newman; directed by Donna Ray; percussion and sound recording by Mark Gordon; filmed at The Cock Hotel, Stony Stratford, 22/3/18 with guest parodists: Faeries, Fay Roberts, Phil Alexander, Justin Thyme and Richard Frost.